HOW TO TURN ... H

Wealth is often measure... s
YOUR LIFE. The power to ... r
best self is the most val... ever own. When you embrace gratitude, you unlock limitless potential, opening doors to even greater opportunities. This is your foundation to dream, build, and accomplish. **YOUR TIME IS NOW!** The moment you believe in your potential, the world begins to open up for you.

True wealth takes many forms, and each of them plays a vital role in shaping the life you desire:

WEALTH = $, WEALTH = , WEALTH =

- **Wealth includes money** and the ability to earn, manage, and grow it, providing the resources to turn your dreams into reality.

- **Wealth is also your inner world**, your mindset, growth, and the investment you make in yourself. It is your greatest and most valuable asset.

- **Wealth is health**, both physical and mental, as a strong and resilient body, paired with a grateful mind, fuels your energy and determination to achieve your highest goals.

In this book, we will discuss all the types of wealth mentioned earlier: Financial Wealth, Inner Wealth, and Health & Gratitude.

Focus on improving, not proving.

© 2025 BY DARIUSZ ROMANOVSKI
ALL RIGHTS RESERVED.

This work is protected under international copyright laws, and violations may result in legal action.

Thank you for supporting my work and respecting the effort that went into creating this book.

Feel free to share photos of the book or its content on social media to inspire others, just be sure to credit the author: @mylifexsoul / Dariusz Romanovski.

THIS PRODUCT IS ONLY FOR PERSONAL USE.

Commercial use or distribution of any part of this book without author permission is prohibited. For any other uses, please reach out to me for permission.

No part of this book may be reproduced, stored, or shared without prior written permission from the author. This includes unauthorized digital copies, file sharing, or audio recordings of its content.

This book was designed using Canva under a commercial license.
Canva, as a tool and platform, provided the space. Creators shared their work and art, and through vision, and through God-given talents and vision, I shaped these elements into a meaningful and intentional creation.

Grateful for the opportunity and to the creators whose art became part of my deep creation, inspired by a mission to leave a legacy that lasts for generations, shared with you.

Genre: Self-Help / Motivational.

Bibliographic information is available on the Lithuanian Integral Library Information System (LIBIS) portal ibiblioteka.lt

ISBN: 978-609-08-0801-6 (paperback)
ISBN: 978-609-08-0802-3 (PDF)

What's the Real Problem?

Have you ever looked at your life and wondered, "What's holding me back from the life I want?"

You know there's more out there, more potential, more success, more meaning, but something always seems to hold you back. Maybe it's fear? Fear of failing, fear of stepping out of your comfort zone, or maybe it's that quiet doubt whispering, "What if I'm not enough?"

This book was written for moments like yours, when you feel stuck and uncertain of how to move forward. It's not about searching for quick results or waiting for a miraculous transformation. It's about embracing the power of small, purposeful steps that can change everything in your life.

Inside, you'll find real answers, practical guidance, and a roadmap to help you face your fears, break free from the patterns holding you back, and finally move toward the life you've been dreaming of.

Dear Soul, so many of us hope and pray to be heard. I prayed that each person would be heard, that their requests would be heeded. I've dedicated time I can never get back to this journey, driven by the belief that I can make a difference, and that you will listen to your inner voice and unleash the strength and potential that already lives within you.

For those motivated to unleash their inner potential and truly LEVEL-UP their life, this book will guide you easily, step by step.

The "new me" begins with
accepting yourself and your entire life story.

You may see yourself as "SELF-MADE,"
but every struggle, every critic, and every believer
along the way has shaped your growth and success.

Strive to be known as a grateful person.

CONTENTS

In this book, we will discuss all the types of wealth mentioned earlier: Financial Wealth, Inner Wealth, and Health & Gratitude.

Why This Book? NEXT-LEVEL YOU!

- **Breaking Free from Paralysis:** I've noticed that many people feel stuck, saying things like, "I don't know what I want." Makes sense? This book will help you break free from the chaos and confusion, cutting through the fog and guiding you toward clarity, purpose, and action. I'm here to help close the gap between your current reality and the life you've always dreamed of. After all, this is the answer you've been silently seeking.
- **Easy to Read and Interactive MATRIX GAME:** Say goodbye to traditional, boring self-improvement books! With its innovative, game-inspired design, this book turns learning into an engaging, interactive experience. Motivational visuals and a unique level-up system will keep you moving forward on your journey.
- **Step-by-Step Transformation:** This book breaks your journey into manageable steps, empowering you to take action alongside your created character, leading to meaningful life changes.
- **A Problem Solver, Not a "Motivational Guru":** This book fills a gap in self-development by offering a fresh, innovative approach. It's not just another motivational read. This is a practical guide focused on action, immersing you in an interactive journey of personal growth.
- **Empowerment for Introverts:** If you're an introvert, this book provides a unique path for you to connect with your character, build confidence, and take meaningful actions outside of your comfort zone.
- **A True Moment of Awakening:** There was a time in my life when everything felt chaotic, even the decisions I made. I've learned that each challenge carried valuable experience and lessons. My life has always been focused on transformation, yet everything changed after foot surgery. To learn more about the story behind the book, turn to page 188.

START NOW!

To finish a 200-page book, try breaking it down into manageable steps. Read just 7 pages a day instead of pushing yourself to get through 100 pages at once.

In 30 days, you'll not only have finished this book, but you'll have built a consistent habit — a true discipline.

In this transformative adventure, you'll:

- **Create Your Character:** Design a persona that embodies your strengths and aspirations, then activate it in the matrix game of life, where your transformation begins.
- **Face Your Fears:** Travel through dark forests of uncertainty and uncover the roots of your fears, anxieties, and obstacles. It's time to confront what's holding you back.
- **Meet the Wise Man:** Gain valuable wisdom and confidence from a mentor who will guide you through life's challenges, revealing different types of wealth. His mission is to provide purpose, fulfillment, and personal growth that can transform your life.
- **Find the Dragon of Wishes:** Uncover the secrets that reveal the hidden truths within you and turn your deepest desires into reality.

Listen to Your Mind or

In life, we constantly face a choice: follow the mind or the soul? Exist or live? Most rely on the mind yet remain unfulfilled. That's because the mind isn't designed for happiness. It seeks comfort, avoids risks, and resists change.

The soul, however, desires more. It seeks joy, purpose, dreams, goals, and growth. Listening to it means stepping into the unknown and embracing uncertainty. This is where inner conflict begins. The mind resists and fills you with doubt saying "You're not good enough. You'll fail," because it doesn't believe in dreams, only analyzing past experiences and fearing the unknown.

This resistance leads to procrastination, anxiety, and self-doubt, draining your energy and leaving you stuck. Eventually, it can lead to panic attacks, depression, and emptiness as the mind cannot recharge you like the soul and instead drains your energy.

But you can break free by challenging negativity and affirming, "Everything will work out. I will at least try. I trust." Suddenly, you begin to see meaning in struggles and hidden opportunities. As you connect more with your soul, energy returns naturally.

The soul speaks through intuition, emotions, and inspiration. Have you ever noticed your best ideas come when you're at peace or in motion? That's your soul guiding you. The mind analyzes and doubts, but the soul knows. When you align with it, something shifts. Maybe even a shiver is running through your body right now?

Self-belief, self-awareness, and self-acceptance form the foundation of your dream life, empowering you to create the reality you've always desired. Dreams come true when belief is supported by action. The right people, ideas, and opportunities begin to appear. Sometimes, the shift begins with something simple, like a walk outside, a deep breath, or the small but powerful act of choosing trust over doubt.

Now is the time to trust! Let your soul lead, and when fear fills your mind, remind yourself, “Why is this important to me?” Answer it, and this will create powerful synergy to achieve and attract what you desire.

The Choice Effect

The power is in your hands! Will you continue to accept the life you've known, or will you step into the limitless possibilities that lie ahead? If the idea of human potential interests you, then let's take the first step toward discovery.

Every day, we make choices that determine how our life will be tomorrow. Our actions today shape our future.

If I am too lazy today to invest in my personal development, I shouldn't ask myself tomorrow, "Why don't I have it?" Reflect on your past actions to understand the current results of your choices. It will become clear why you might lack something in the present.

If you didn't take action today to expand your mindset, grow your confidence, or invest in your future, then don't question tomorrow, "Why aren't things different?"

Consistently making choices that align with your personal goals builds positive momentum. This book will help you remove fear and obstacles from your life, leaving only an open door to your dreams and goals. After the first step, the path ahead will unfold with clarity and purpose.

If you've chosen this book and are reading it, it means you're ready for something more. This is a meaningful step in your journey. **Are you loyal to your desire?**

Why "The Magic of Goals"?

At the core of every transformation is the goal. Goals are not just markers of achievement but powerful catalysts for change. When we set clear, intentional goals, we unlock the ability to shape our reality. Goals provide direction, focus, and drive, guiding us to places we never imagined.

The magic comes not only from achieving our goals but also from the journey itself. As we strive toward our goals, the right people, opportunities, experiences, and lessons begin to align with us. Through this process, we become the architects of our own future.

Invitation to the Journey

I extend a warm invitation to you, my curious companion, to join me on this transformative journey of self-discovery and growth. As you turn the pages of this book, prepare to explore new ideas, challenge old beliefs, and uncover the limitless potential within you. Your participation is not passive. It is an active engagement with the game of life, where every decision you make and action you take contributes to your evolution as a person.

As we enter the chapter titled *"Your Life, Your Game,"* the character you've created steps into a world full of opportunities. The path ahead is clear, the rules are simple, and the journey awaits your first move. Prepare to venture into the unknown, where growth and discovery are the true destinations.

Let's move forward with curiosity, courage, and commitment to continuous growth!

The Chinese philosopher Lao Tzu once said, "The journey of a thousand miles begins with a single step."

From Chaos to Clarity

Children learn to fear failure early on, often hearing phrases like "Don't try," "Sit quietly," "Why can't you be normal," and "Don't reveal your beauty or talent because you'll be criticized."

When children absorb these messages, they struggle in various aspects of life, including relationships, as they become unsure of how to behave or what to say. They may seek approval, fear being themselves, or ignore their own voice. Remember, those who imposed these limitations were once children too.

Life is like a game, full of choices. It's a game where you search for words among scattered letters and ask yourself questions:

"What is my calling?"
"What is the path of my soul?"
"What is wrong with me?"

This is the process of life, finding the words among the letters. When you find enough words, you feel the connection. Words become sentences, sentences become thoughts, thoughts become actions, and actions become results. When you exhale and open your eyes, you become fully who you are and accept it within yourself, and that is beautiful.

When chaos turns into clarity, life becomes energized, and goals become attainable.

Change is the key to progress. Wanting something new requires doing something new. Achieving our goals requires bold action, and through that action, we create meaningful change in our lives and within ourselves.

Every goal you set, every vision you work towards, reflects the person you are becoming: the unique qualities, values, and mindset that define you. To create lasting change, start by appreciating who you are now. True transformation begins the moment you accept your current self. This book will guide you through that transformation.

"Share this message, uplift others, and create change. Together, we grow. Mention @mylifexsoul in your story!"

YOU CAN DO IT, YOU CAN DO IT, YOU CAN DO IT, YOU CAN DO IT!
YOU CAN DO IT, YOU CAN DO IT, YOU CAN DO IT, YOU CAN DO IT!
YOU CAN DO IT, YOU CAN DO IT, YOU CAN DO IT, YOU CAN DO IT!

YOU CAN DO IT, YOU CAN DO IT, YOU CAN DO IT, YOU CAN DO IT!
YOU CAN DO IT, YOU CAN DO IT, YOU CAN DO IT, YOU CAN DO IT!
YOU CAN DO IT, YOU CAN DO IT, YOU CAN DO IT, YOU CAN DO IT!

Part of the Story: Before the Journey

There was a time in my life when everything felt chaotic, even the decisions I made, though each brought valuable experience and lessons. My life has always been focused on transformation, but everything changed after foot surgery. I had six weeks to recover, and I decided to use this time wisely. I found myself at a crossroads, questioning my worth and purpose: Who am I? What do I really want?

In that moment, I realized that I needed to take control and help myself. I began exploring old notebooks filled with random notes, thoughts, philosophy, and dreams, trying to make sense of it all.

It was a moment of chaos, but also a moment of awakening. I recalled how I had been constantly praying, "God, act through me," and in that realization, I began to understand things more deeply. I reignited the spark of my childhood dreams, not just for myself, but for the inspirational legacy I wanted to leave behind. I needed to organize my thoughts and dreams to find clarity. It was about unlocking a deeper purpose and aligning my life with my true desires. At first, I set out to create this book not as a guide for others, but as a guide for myself, but surprisingly it evolved into something much bigger.

God said, "believe and receive." Combining creativity, God-given talents, storytelling, and inspiration from the profound lessons life has taught me, I felt inspired to create this book as both a self-help and motivational guide, uniquely presented as an adventure through your own character's journey.

Learn more about the story behind the book on page 188.

CHAPTER 1: THE START OF YOUR JOURNEY

Installing 1% 

What will I do today to become stronger tomorrow?

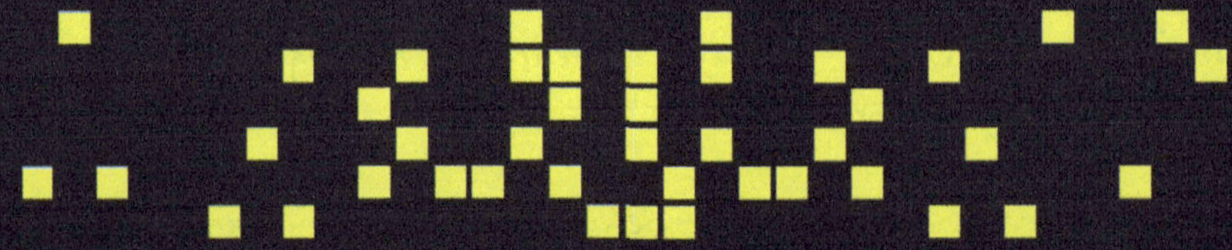

You're brave for starting this journey – this adventure!

This book is your invitation to level up. It's not just about reading—it's about experiencing. Each chapter is crafted to guide you, challenge you, and inspire you to uncover your purpose, master your mindset, and create the life you've always imagined.

Think of it as a treasure map to your true potential. The tools, strategies, and lessons in these pages are here to help you break free from chaos, silence your doubts, and awaken the hero within you.

Are you ready to take the first step on your journey?

The Quest Begins

Every great journey begins with a choice:
Who do I want to become?

Just as an experienced gamer customizes their avatar for a virtual adventure, you will embark on a journey of self-discovery to shape the character who will guide you through challenges and lead you to success. This journey begins with reflection on your strengths, weaknesses, past wins, and lessons learned on the way.

This path is about embracing your unique qualities, celebrating every small victory, and learning from each setback. Remember, your imperfections are not obstacles. They are the very stepping stones shaping you into the person you are destined to become. Trust the journey and keep moving forward.

The world will present challenges that will test your courage and resilience. Life's twists and turns may not always make sense, but your quest and your *"why"* will be the light that guides you forward. With courage in your heart and determination in your mind, you can overcome any obstacle. Each struggle will shape you into a stronger, wiser version of yourself.

As you step into this journey, remember that the character you create is not just an idea. It is you! This is not about pretending to be someone else. It is about stepping fully into the person you have always been capable of becoming. Every choice you make, every habit you build, and every challenge you face with resolve will bring you closer to mastering the game of life.

Let this journey be one of intention, growth, and purpose. **The hero inside you is ready.** Rise with confidence, take bold action, and uncover the unique adventure that's waiting for you to discover.

A Letter to Your Future Self

Take a moment to write a message to the person you will become. What do you want to achieve? How do you want to grow? Be honest and bold, knowing this note will remind you of where you started and guide you on your journey ahead. Write it as if your future self is reading it for the first time, because this is the moment that will shape everything to come.

Set your intentions, dreams, and goals clearly on this page. Reflect on where you are now and who you truly want to be. This isn't just a note. It's a statement of your potential, a promise to your future self. It's the spark that will ignite your transformation, the first step towards a life you've always imagined.

Believe in Yourself

YOU CAN DO IT, YOU CAN DO IT, YOU CAN DO IT, YOU CAN DO IT!
YOU CAN DO IT, YOU CAN DO IT, YOU CAN DO IT, YOU CAN DO IT!
YOU CAN DO IT, YOU CAN DO IT, YOU CAN DO IT, YOU CAN DO IT!

2

YOU CAN DO IT, YOU CAN DO IT, YOU CAN DO IT, YOU CAN DO IT!
YOU CAN DO IT, YOU CAN DO IT, YOU CAN DO IT, YOU CAN DO IT!
YOU CAN DO IT, YOU CAN DO IT, YOU CAN DO IT, YOU CAN DO IT!

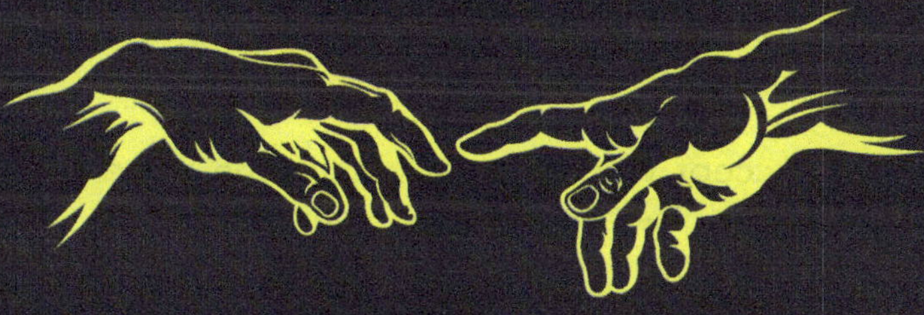

CHAPTER 2.1:
DESIGN YOUR CHARACTER

Installing 2%

The Soul's Whisper: A Hidden Start

You are not just a body. You are a unique individual, a soul filled with unrevealed potential, as well as incredible gifts. Recognizing your individuality and even your weirdness is the key to unlocking your freedom and creating the life you've always desired. The uniqueness you hold is your greatest power, setting you apart from the crowd and enabling you to create a life that truly reflects who you are.

As you journey through this book, you will experience a unique feeling, one that is yours to define and appreciate: a feeling of clarity, purpose, and empowerment.

The more you accept who you are within, the more you'll unlock your own potential. The answers you seek are already within you. However, the noise of modern life, overwhelming fears, and past experiences often overshadow your true voice.

We frequently desire many things but focus more on the "how." This often leads us to abandon our dreams, labeling them as "impossible" and limiting our aspirations.

Your task is not to figure out *"HOW,"* but to clearly understand *"WHAT"* you want. Be open to discovering and embracing the information and opportunities that will reveal the *"HOW."* Trust fully in your journey, and allow yourself to explore with an open heart and curious mind.

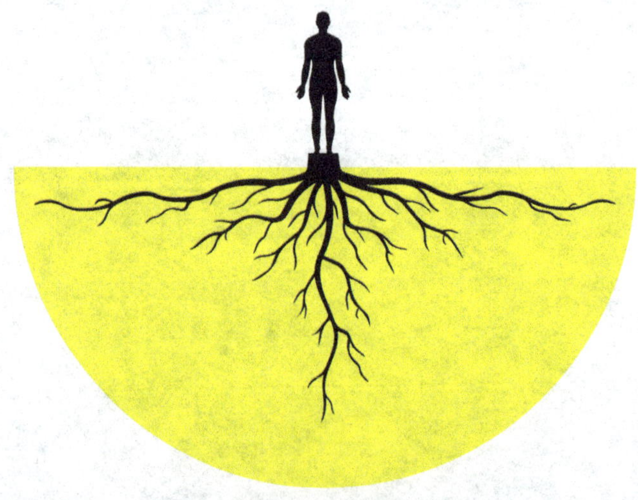

Exploring Your Strengths

Your strengths are the foundation of who you are, defining your character and unlocking your potential for success.

Take a moment to pause and reflect on your journey so far. What victories have shaped you? What skills and talents have you gained over time? Think about the situations where you feel fully engaged and driven, able to accomplish more than you thought possible. These moments highlight your true capabilities, recognize them and use them to level up to even greater achievements.

- **Review Your Achievements:** Think back to moments when you felt unstoppable. What strengths helped you achieve those successes? Recognize the natural talents that helped you get there and consider how you can leverage them to reach even greater heights of success.
- **Get Feedback from Others:** Talk to the people around you about what they admire most about you. Their perspective can reveal strengths you might not have noticed. How do their views compare to how you see yourself?
- **Understand Your Personality:** Your personality shapes how you approach challenges and view the world. What strengths drive your success? Recognize how these qualities contribute to your achievements. You can also take the *"16 Personalities"* test to explore your strengths in more detail.
- **Fuel Your Passions with Strengths:** When your strengths align with your deepest interests, success follows. What excites you?
- **Appreciate Your Worth:** Acknowledge your unique strengths and the progress you've made. Recognize your worth, and know that there's even more potential waiting for you.

Dear Reader, be kind to yourself. Self-acceptance is the key to unlocking your power to reach your fullest potential.

I CAN DO IT!

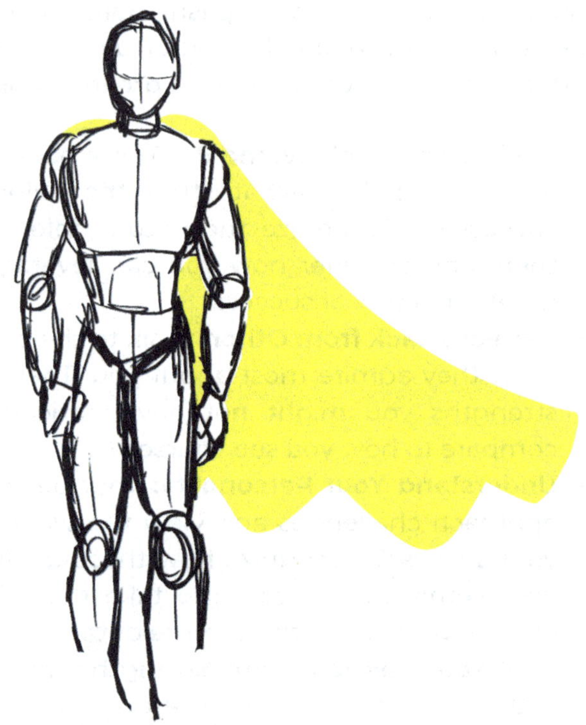

YES! YOU CAN DO IT!
YES! YOU CAN DO IT!
YES! YOU CAN DO IT!

Strength is the power to influence and shape your own life.

"Share this message, uplift others, and create change. Together, we grow. Mention @mylifexsoul in your story!"

Identifying Your Weaknesses

While your strengths define your character, your weaknesses offer opportunities for growth. Be honest with yourself as you reflect on areas where you struggle or fall short. What challenges are you facing? What obstacles are holding you back? Acknowledge these weaknesses with courage and self-awareness. Each challenge you face is a chance to grow and improve.

- **Transform Challenges into Growth:** Identify the struggles that are holding you back. Facing them is the first step to growth. Understanding these challenges helps you take control and find solutions. With each step, you'll gain confidence and develop the resilience needed to move forward. Accept the journey, knowing that growth often comes from confronting what holds you back.
- **Reflect on Setbacks:** Look at past failures as lessons. Every setback offers an opportunity for a comeback if you learn from it.
- **Seek Feedback:** Ask for honest feedback from trusted people. Their perspective can reveal areas for improvement you might not see. Listen carefully to their insights, as they can help you identify blind spots and guide your personal growth.
- **Dive Into Self-Reflection:** Dive deep into your thoughts and behaviors. Recognizing patterns that hold you back is crucial for progress.
- **Facing Change:** Accepting your weaknesses with courage is the first step toward transformation and growth.
- **Level Up:** Address your weaknesses with determination. View challenges as opportunities to evolve, pushing yourself to learn, adapt, and become stronger with each experience. Each step forward, no matter how small, is progress.

Dear Reader, anyone can improve by just 1% each day. Progress is made step by step, not all at once. The choice is yours, shaped by your challenges and desires. Success is yours to create, make it purposeful and unique to you.

Space for Your Notes:

True success is found when you rise above your own limitations and conquer your inner battles.

Level up

The truth is, it's not about how smart you are or how many skills you possess. It's about what you do with what you have. Success isn't just for the gifted or the talented. Success isn't for those who wait. It's for those who take action and make things happen.

Think about it, success isn't about never failing. It's about learning from each failure and moving forward with more determination.

Picture a baby trying to walk. It doesn't stand up and get it right on the first try, does it? No. It stumbles, it falls, but it keeps trying. And eventually, it walks. If that baby had stopped at the first fall, there would be no walking. But that baby knows something we sometimes forget: failure is just part of the process.

And that's where you're at right now. You may have failed, you may have fallen, but you can stand again. And you will! Because the version of you that achieves everything you desire is already inside. All it takes is a little persistence, a little courage, and the willingness to get back up after each setback.

Hey, future you!

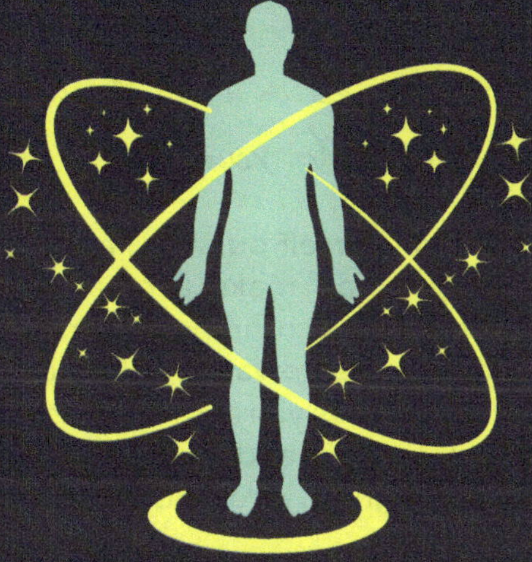

I believe in you! I believe in your ability to turn every setback into a stepping stone. I believe in your ability to rise higher, to learn, to grow, and to become the person you've always known you were meant to be.

Your desires are a reflection of the person you're becoming. They show you that who you are today is not who you're meant to be. The version of you who accomplishes those dreams has qualities, habits, and courage you haven't unlocked yet.

So, let's get to work, together. We're about to create that future you, the one who is living the life you've always dreamed of.

Are you ready to step into that person?

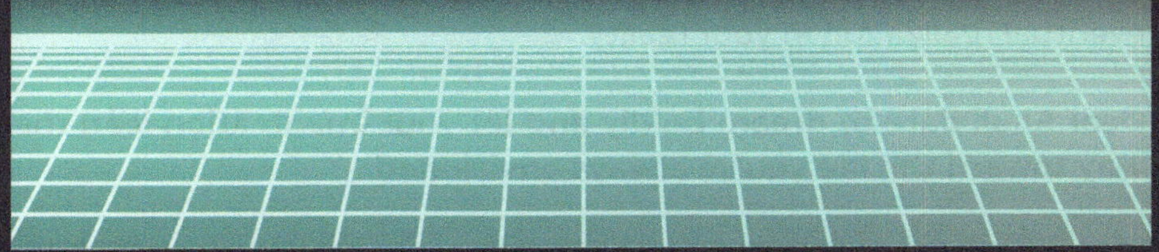

Exploring Your Dream Life

Take a moment to close your eyes and imagine a life where anything is possible. Picture yourself waking up each morning, feeling excited and inspired, knowing that the day ahead is filled with endless opportunities for joy, fulfillment, and success.

What do you see in this dream life?
What do you feel?

In this vision, do you find yourself pursuing a career that aligns with your passions, where you can make a meaningful impact in the world? Or perhaps you envision running your own business, leading a team of driven individuals toward a shared vision of success. Maybe your dream life includes vibrant relationships, surrounded by friends and family who uplift and empower you, creating deep connections filled with laughter, love, and unforgettable memories.

Imagine a life where you experience inner peace, knowing that your actions align with your values and purpose. You feel gratitude for everything around you, appreciating the beauty and joy in each moment.

As you continue to visualize your dream life, allow yourself to explore the details and nuances that bring it to life. What activities do you engage in? What goals do you pursue? What impact do you have on the world around you?

Take a moment to write down your reflections and insights, capturing the essence of your dream life on paper. Use descriptive language to paint a vivid picture for yourself, allowing your imagination to run wild as you explore the possibilities.

Remember, your dream life is yours to create. Taking the time to envision it with clarity and intention truly plants the seeds for its eventual realization in your reality.

Dear Soul, dare to dream boldly and let your imagination lead the way toward the life you've always envisioned.

Who Must I Become to Get There?

"We are what we think, all that we arise with our thoughts, with our thoughts we make the world."
— Buddha

If you want to live a different life than before, you must do things you've never done before. All energy vibrates at a certain frequency. So, you are vibrating at a certain frequency, and everything you want or don't want is also vibrating at a certain frequency.

To raise your vibrational frequency, you need to believe that all your desires are possible. The best way to maintain this belief is by staying connected to your faith. Many answers come from action, not from thinking. You can start from nothing and from nothing the path will begin. You are a victim of the rules you live by.

1. Mission:

Define Your Higher Self:
Even if you only answer a couple of questions, it's already progress.

- **Core Values:** What values guide you?
- **Mindset:** How do you view the world?
- **Lifestyle:** What does your ideal day look like?
- **Purpose:** What impact do you aim to make?
- **Confidence:** How do you trust yourself and take bold actions?
- **Qualities:** What strengths make you inspiring?
- **Ambitions:** What goals are you dedicated to achieving?
- **Resilience:** How do you handle challenges and setbacks?
- **Environment:** Where do you live, and why?
- **Money Mindset:** How do you view and use money?
- **Growth:** How do you keep learning and growing?
- **Relationships:** How do you treat others?
- **Health:** How do you maintain physical and mental well-being?
- **Expression:** How do you express your creativity?
- **Legacy:** What impact do you wish to leave?
- **Time Management:** How do you prioritize your time?
- **Self-Reflection:** How do you stay connected to your inner self?

Space for Your Notes:

Remember, everything is energy, and every energy vibrates at a frequency. People with similar intentions connect on the same frequency. Love is a frequency, success is a frequency of action and faith, and even fear is a frequency. Align your energy with what you desire, and watch the world around you shift in response.

"Share this message, uplift others, and create change. Together, we grow. Mention @mylifexsoul in your story!"

Now or Someday?

Now! Even though you think you're not quite ready for it. Nobody cares anymore, and probably nobody will notice that not everything is 100% perfect. Honestly, nothing will ever be 100% perfect anyway, so you better start now! The present moment is a wonderful thing, massively undervalued, there is no better way to act than to start right away.

You will always find a way, or you will find excuses if you don't. When you say ***"I can,"*** opportunities and solutions appear, whether through others or by discovering them yourself. The most important thing is that you receive help. But when you say ***"I can't,"*** it's as if you've closed the door to help.

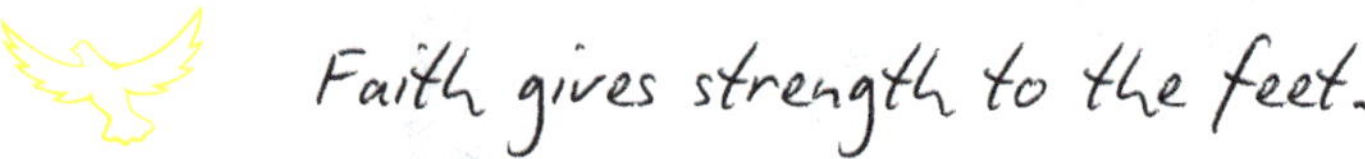

There are many people in the world living the life you only dream of. **Many of them are not as wonderful and talented as YOU!** The secret of their success is that they decided to strive for their own. They didn't listen to old excuses, they changed their bad habits, and they spit in the face of everything. This decision is non-negotiable.

When I made the decision to pursue this goal, I committed to becoming the kind of person who can achieve anything I set my mind to, whether it's building meaningful relationships, mastering a skill, or creating an impact in the world. Once you understand what is possible for you and decide to pursue it, there will be more opportunities to make it happen.

Change is a weakness < Change is a strength.

YOUR FAITH - THE KEY

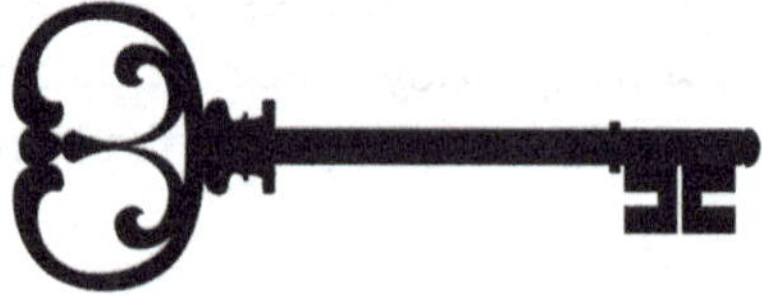

"Share this message, uplift others, and create change.
Together, we grow. Mention @mylifexsoul in your story!"

The answer is ACTION - ACTION - ACTION.
Follow your vision and achieve it!
Faith is the courage to wholeheartedly
believe in what is not yet seen.

Level
up

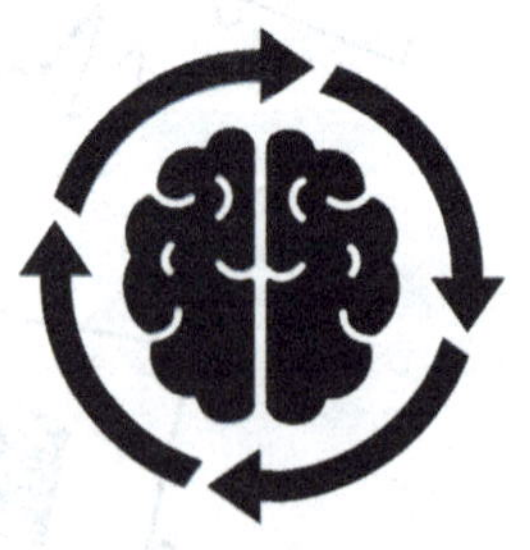

Breathe in
breathe out
let it in

CHAPTER 2.2:
IGNITE YOUR INNER POWER

Installing 3% 

Awaken the Superhero Within You!

You can no longer act like a victim and let life be controlled by circumstances, **you can act like a SUPERHERO!** Create a life where you wake up every morning and have unexpected happiness for being who you are.

Keep moving, keep sacrificing, keep overcoming challenges, keep improving. You have passed one level, you have moved on to the next, take the next step. What matters is the willingness to move forward and overcome them, not to retreat into the comfort zone that separates those who succeed from those who are stagnating.

All life is progress and EVOLUTION.

I am strong and confident, guided by the energy of the Almighty. With God and the Universe supporting me, I keep growing, learning, and evolving. When my mind and body align, I unleash even greater power. I stay focused on my goals, take every action that moves me forward, and leave no space for doubt. I commit fully, knowing I will make it happen. I remain open to new opportunities, trusting that everyone receives exactly what they need to succeed.

"Your beliefs become your thoughts, your thoughts become your words, your words become your actions, your actions become your habits, your habits become your values, your values become your destiny." — Gandhi

Look! Your "***reality***" becomes possible. How wonderful is that, huh?

The world around you is a reflection of the energy you put out. When you choose to believe in your power, in your ability to rise, the Universe responds. The doors open, and what seemed impossible becomes within your reach. You've already started this journey. You've taken that first step. Now, stay focused and keep moving forward.

The key to your success is simple. Keep your focus on the goal but stay open to the lessons along the way. Sometimes, the greatest gifts come in the most unexpected forms. And as you push through the challenges, remember that every setback is simply a setup for your comeback.

"No one else can ever write your life story for you. It's yours to create."

— Unknown

You're writing your story, and each day you're making it better. You're building a future you can be proud of, brick by brick, choice by choice. There's no limit to what you can achieve when you believe in yourself and trust that everything you need is already within you.

You're unstoppable! Keep going. Amazing things are waiting for you!

"Share this message, uplift others, and create change. Together, we grow. Mention @mylifexsoul in your story!"

"Every moment is a choice."
— Unknown

Every moment is a choice. In each moment, you hold the power to decide who you want to be, what you want to achieve, and how you want to show up in the world. Life is not a series of events happening to you, but a collection of choices you make. Choose wisely, for every decision, no matter how small, shapes your path toward the life you desire. The future you want starts with the choices you make today.

"Share this message, uplift others, and create change. Together, we grow. Mention @mylifexsoul in your story!"

THIS IS YOU AND YOUR NEEDS

Recognition and appreciation

Health and wellness

comfort

self-actualization

Safety

Creativity and expression

love

Privacy

Financial security

social connection

independence

.etc

Emotional well-being

Overall, meeting basic human needs is essential for survival, health, happiness, and fulfillment. It lays the foundation for individuals to thrive and lead fulfilling lives.

THIS IS YOUR WHEEL OF LIFE

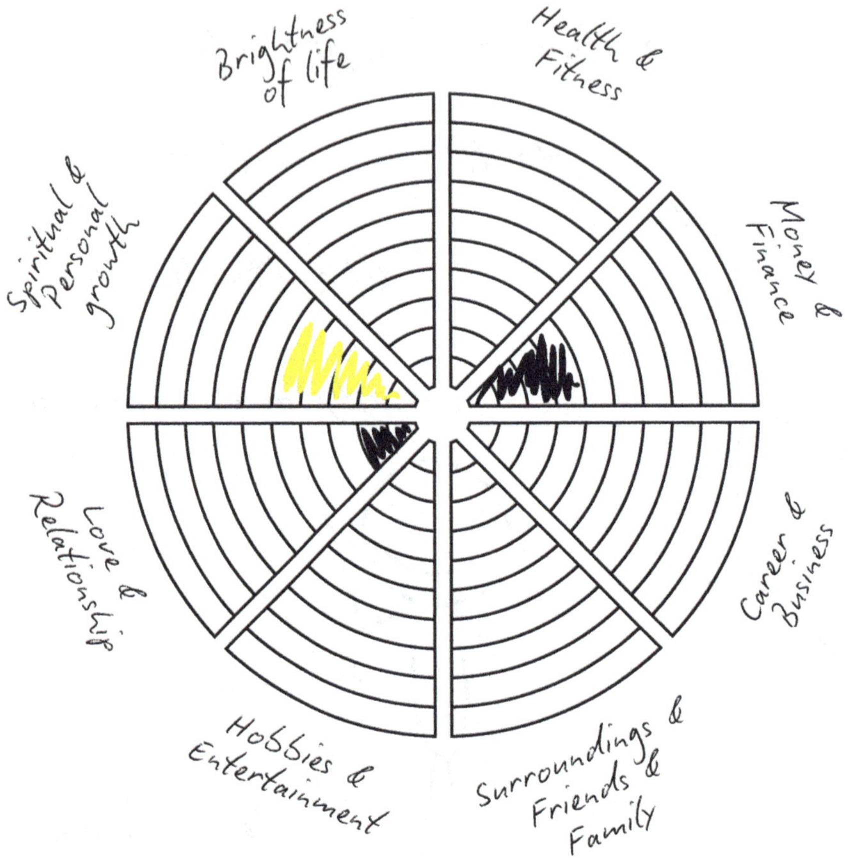

Analyze your life according to the circle of life, which areas lag and which dominate the most? Where would you like to improve?

I believe in you and the life you want. The only thing standing between you and a better version of yourself, your next level, is the story you tell yourself: ***"Why can't I get it?"***

Take a moment to reflect with the Wheel of Life Exercise. Simply search online for a free version.

Level up

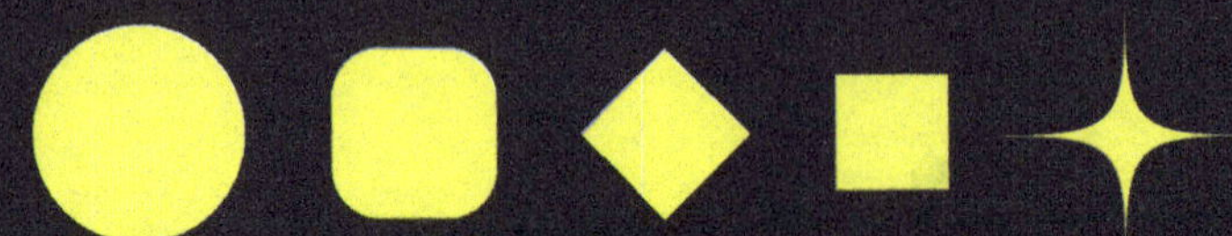

CHAPTER 2.3:
SUCCESS: YOUR REFLECTION

Installing 4%

Success Is Built on Character

Character leads to success. A person's character, developed under pressure and shaped by inner strength, determines their path. The energy you radiate reflects who you are, and that's what draws others toward you. Authenticity and inner power are the keys to lasting success, both in relationships and in life. Character is formed through the journey, shaped by life's challenges and experiences. Success is determined not so much by external factors as by the internal ones. Any door will open before you if you are strong and full of energy. Inner strength is the key.

Unleash the Leader within You!

The "old witch of failure" loses all her strength and barriers, giving way to success. Failure and defeat cannot resist persistence.

It's not a question of whether you're a loser or not. It's how many tries you need to get the results you want. I know that I will do some things well and some things badly, and neither reflects my value as a human being. This is called unconditional self-acceptance.

What I've learned is that the mistakes, judgments, and criticism of others show that I have taken risks and seized opportunities to grow. To be imperfect and make mistakes is to be human.

It was enough to make them believe it...
(the medicine Placeba)

I am strong and powerful, I can handle all the difficulties that come my way. I look at defeat only as life lessons to be learned. I don't give up just because things get hard, I am happy and grateful, and boldly I choose to move forward with unwavering confidence, and yes, I am the unstoppable leader of my life!

At
the heart
of every success are
mistakes, failures, and losses.
The pyramid of success is made of
the stones of these failures. Don't complain but act.

"Share this message, uplift others, and create change.
Together, we grow. Mention @mylifexsoul in your story!"

Nothing has changed in my life until I change myself. I can help myself! I have decided that from now on I will take full responsibility for my life and everything that happens to me. I am the master of my destiny. This is my life and if I don't do something to change it, it will stay like this forever.

7 Principles of Leadership in personal life:

1. **Know Yourself:** To lead others, you must first understand who you are. Reflect on your strengths, weaknesses, values, and beliefs. Self-awareness empowers you to make decisions aligned with your true self, inspiring others to do the same.
2. **Define Purpose:** Your purpose is your compass. Knowing your core values and what truly matters allows you to set meaningful goals and navigate life with clarity. When you're aligned with your purpose, everything else falls into place.
3. **Vision:** A clear vision drives your actions. Picture your ideal future and set goals that align with that vision. Vision is your internal roadmap, guiding decisions today that lead to tomorrow's success. Act with purpose, knowing where you're headed.
4. **Develop Resilience:** Life will challenge you, but your resilience shapes your response. Build mental toughness to bounce back from setbacks and face challenges with courage. Resilience turns failures into lessons and obstacles into growth opportunities.
5. **Practice Empathy:** Leaders lead with kindness. See things from different viewpoints, listen with care, and offer support. This builds trust and significantly strengthens your leadership impact.
6. **Accountability:** Leadership is responsibility. Own your actions and their effects on yourself and others. Stay true to your values and take credit for both successes and failures. Responsibility builds trust and sets the example for those you lead.
7. **Continuous Growth:** Leadership is a journey of growth. Commit to learning, confront discomfort, and value constructive criticism. Push beyond your comfort zone. Every step forward brings you closer to becoming a stronger leader.

1. “The best way to find yourself is to lose yourself in the service of others.” – Mahatma Gandhi
2. “Do not go where the path may lead, go instead where there is no path and leave a trail.” – Ralph Waldo Emerson
3. “The best way to predict the future is to create it.” – Peter Drucker
4. “The only limit to our realization of tomorrow is our doubts of today.” – Franklin D. Roosevelt
5. “What you get by achieving your goals is not as important as what you become by achieving your goals.” – Zig Ziglar
6. “Our lives begin to end the day we become silent about things that matter.” – Martin Luther King Jr.
7. “The only thing standing between you and your goal is the story you keep telling yourself as to why you can’t achieve it.” – Jordan Belfort
8. “It is never too late to be what you might have been.” – George Eliot
9. “Be the change that you wish to see in the world.” – Mahatma Gandhi
10. “Don’t watch the clock, do what it does. Keep going.” – Sam Levenson
11. “It does not matter how slowly you go as long as you do not stop.” – Confucius
12. “In the end, we only regret the chances we didn’t take.” – Lewis Carroll
13. “The secret to getting ahead is getting started.” – Mark Twain
14. “We always think that we’re not ready, but that’s just fear talking.” – Sara Blakely
15. “If you don't understand the details of your business, you are going to fail.” – Jeff Bezos
16. “I’ve failed over and over and over again in my life and that is why I succeed.” – Michael Jordan
17. “It always seems impossible until it’s done.” – Nelson Mandela
18. “The people who are crazy enough to think they can change the world are the ones who do.” – Steve Jobs
19. “You ask me: what are you doing? I’m creating something so inspiring, you’ll find yourself asking: how did you do that?” – Dariusz Romanovski
20. **Your personal quote:** [Space for your quote]

The character was created!

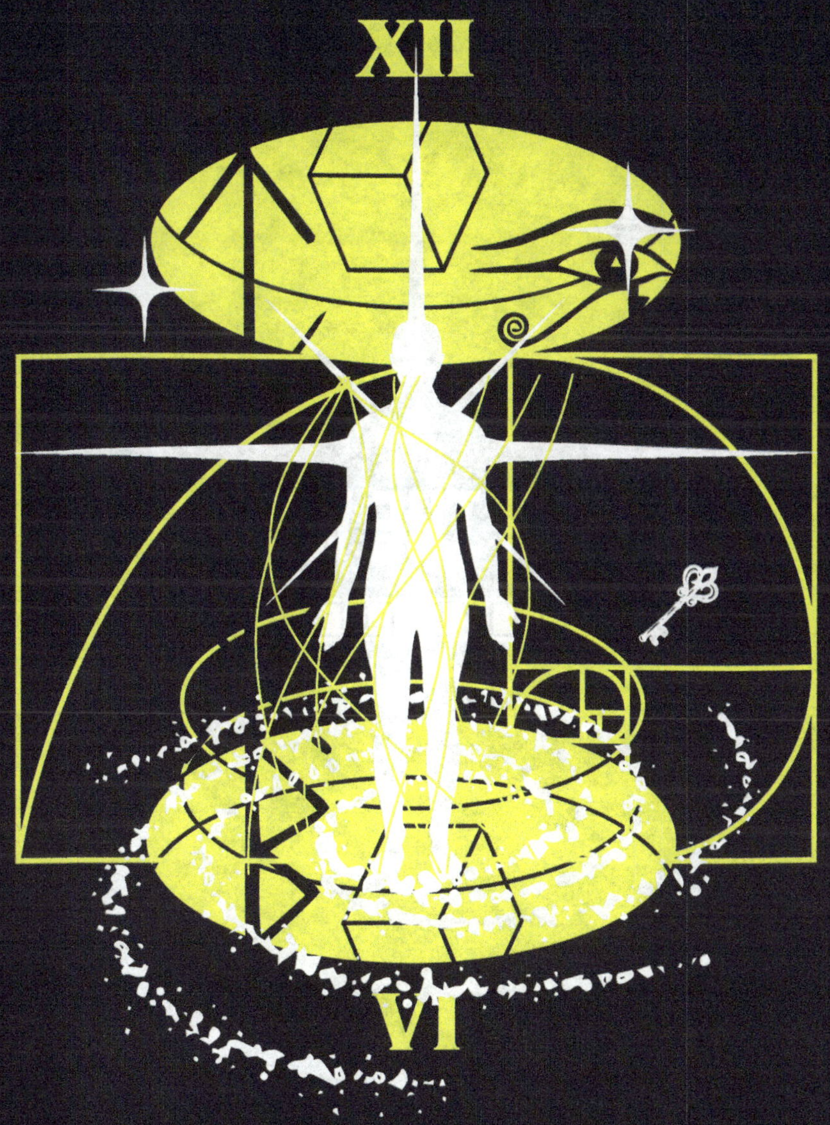

3

ENTER THE WORLD

LOADING...

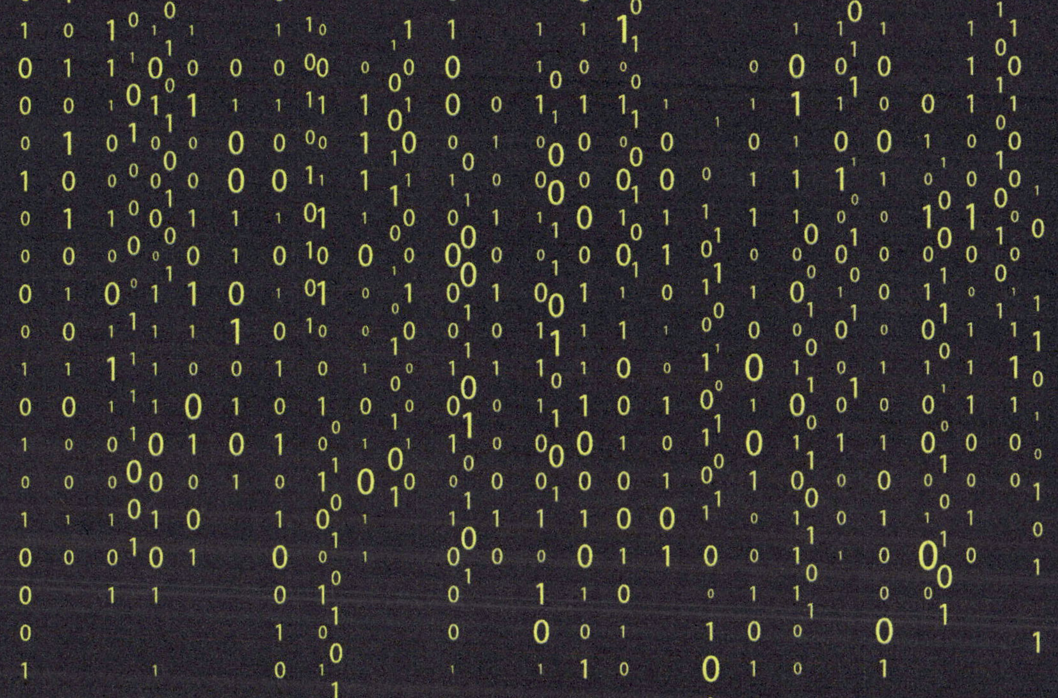

CHAPTER 3:
YOUR LIFE, YOUR GAME

Installing 15%

Mind reset...
10010111 10100101 01001000
CLEAR. DATA RESET. PROCESS COMPLETE.

Life as a Video Game

As the character you've created, you may not yet have the experience or skills of other players in this game. But now that you've taken the first step, you've entered a world full of endless opportunities, quests, and challenges. This world is filled with levels, knowledge, and powerful characters, some stronger and wiser than you. However, through collaboration with others, you can share experiences, exchange tips, and accelerate your progress in this journey. It's like an MMORPG game.

What's your next move?

The universe acts like a loving parent, offering everything you need while testing how you handle it. It gives you the tools to grow, starting with what you have, ensuring you can manage your desires without being overwhelmed. The only real failure is quitting. Every other experience is valuable feedback. Now that you're here, take the time to observe, understand, and adapt to the world around you, so you can confidently shape your own path.

Your character is having thoughts:

- *"Who am I?"*
- *"What am I doing here?"*
- *"I want to have something."*
- *"I must do something."*

The Journey Into the Unknown

The forest ahead of you is not just a physical place. It feels like a threshold between what you know and what is yet to be discovered. Each step feels like a choice, a decision that moves you deeper into the mystery and into the unknown. The shadows of the trees stretch far and deep, making you wonder what they might be hiding. You hear the rustle of leaves and the occasional creak of a branch, almost as if the sounds are echoing your thoughts. Is this place alive with secrets, or is it waiting for me to uncover its story?

The darkness. It's not just around you, it's within you. Your heart beats faster, and a tightness spreads in your stomach. You can't explain it, but it's there. You don't know where you're headed or what's ahead. *You can't see the entire road in front of you.*

Is this the end of my journey, or the start of something far greater?

In life, it's easy to want to know everything at once. We all want to see the future, to have the map to guide us. But sometimes, all you have is the next step. You can't predict the twists and turns ahead, the obstacles and challenges that may arise, the darkness that might suddenly surround you, but you can choose to move forward anyway. Your story is shaped by the choices you make and by taking action, even when the path isn't clear.

The real challenge? Not knowing what's ahead, but the most important thing is to keep moving forward. One step at a time, even when you feel unsure. Because when you trust that your next step is just as important as the last, you'll find your way. The journey has only just begun. Believe and take the first step, you don't have to see all the road, take the first step.

You take a deep breath. This moment feels significant. The unknown lies just ahead, but you can't stay here forever. Something inside you pushes you forward, urging you to step into the forest. You don't know what lies beyond those trees, but you feel that this is where your journey truly begins.

YOU CAN DO IT, YOU CAN DO IT, YOU CAN DO IT, YOU CAN DO IT!
YOU CAN DO IT, YOU CAN DO IT, YOU CAN DO IT, YOU CAN DO IT!
YOU CAN DO IT, YOU CAN DO IT, YOU CAN DO IT, YOU CAN DO IT!

4

YOU CAN DO IT, YOU CAN DO IT, YOU CAN DO IT, YOU CAN DO IT!
YOU CAN DO IT, YOU CAN DO IT, YOU CAN DO IT, YOU CAN DO IT!
YOU CAN DO IT, YOU CAN DO IT, YOU CAN DO IT, YOU CAN DO IT!

CHAPTER 4:
WHAT'S BEHIND FEAR?

Installing 30%

Action defeats fear.

Fear: A Stepping Stone to Growth

On the other side of fear lies your freedom. The main reason people don't reach their goals is fear of failure. However, letting yourself fail means gaining valuable learning experiences. Fear is the starting point of your journey toward your goal. Recognizing fear is the first step in overcoming it.

Some fears, like the fear of communication, can harm self-esteem. Thoughts like "I'm a loser" or "I'm weak" lead to cognitive distortions, reinforcing negative self-beliefs and impacting your actions and emotions. Procrastination and avoidance only build stress and lower confidence. Procrastination happens when you don't see the value in what you're doing or how it connects to your goals.

Remember, fear doesn't define your worth. It's a natural part of being human. What matters is how we respond. Overcoming fear requires patience and persistent effort, but every step forward brings you closer to lasting growth.

Here's a practical approach to tackle your fears:

- **Plan for the Worst:** Write down how you'll handle each fear. Focus on what you can do right now to manage it. Turning it into actionable steps helps you gain control and move forward, instead of being paralyzed by what might happen in the future.
- **Acknowledge Your Fear:** Confront what scares you by writing it down. Identifying your fear reduces its power, turning it from overwhelming to a challenge you can face with confidence.
- **Take Small Steps:** Gradually confront your fears by focusing on one small step at a time. Each small action builds momentum and reduces the power of fear.
- **Seek Support:** Don't carry your fear by yourself. Connect with trusted friends, family, or a professional. Talking it through can provide new perspectives and make it feel more manageable.
- **Be Kind to Yourself:** Fear is natural, accept it and face it step by step. Build a plan and seek support to weaken fear's hold, giving you the courage to pursue your dreams.

The Power of *"Why?"* in Confronting Fear

To effectively face our fears, we must first understand where they come from. The ***"Why Technique?"*** is a powerful method for diving deeper into our emotions and uncovering the true reasons behind our fears.

Example of applying the *"Why Technique?"*

Identify the Fear: **I am afraid of public speaking.**

First Why?:

- **Question:** Why am I afraid of public speaking?
- **Answer:** Because I am afraid of making a mistake and looking foolish.

Second Why?:

- **Question:** Why am I afraid of making a mistake and looking foolish in front of others?
- **Answer:** Because I worry that people will laugh at me or criticize me.

Third Why?:

- **Question:** Why do I worry that people will laugh at me or criticize me?
- **Answer:** Because I want to be respected and valued.

Fourth Why?:

- **Question:** Why do I want to be respected and valued?
- **Answer:** Because I feel confident and happy when I receive approval and validation from others.

Fifth Why?:

- **Question:** Why do I feel confident and happy when I receive approval from others?
- **Answer:**

Because it validates my significance / self-worth.

When you examine your fear, you'll find it's often rooted in the need for approval and recognition. Understanding this allows you to focus on building self-esteem and confidence, helping you face fear with inner strength and reducing your reliance on the approval of others.

As you continue to focus on your inner strength, you'll begin to notice a shift in how you approach challenges. Instead of viewing them as obstacles, you'll see them as opportunities for growth. The more you invest in your self-worth, the more you'll realize that fear is simply a signal for you to step outside your comfort zone and expand your potential.

Each time you overcome a fear, no matter how small, you build momentum, reinforcing your belief in yourself and your abilities. And the best part? You become less dependent on external validation, creating a sense of freedom that fuels your success. The path to confidence is not a straight line, but every step forward is a testament to your inner strength.

As you embrace the power within you, fear no longer holds the same power it once did. It becomes just another signal to keep moving forward, growing stronger, and becoming more aligned with your true potential. Keep trusting yourself, and let your confidence be the compass that guides you toward your dreams.

Keep moving forward, for each step takes you closer to the life you're meant to create. Trust the process, and let it strengthen you. The person you're becoming is already within you, strong, courageous, and capable of achieving all that you desire. The only thing left to do is to keep moving forward. **Go through darkness to light, go through the unknown to your goals.**

YOU CAN DO IT, YOU CAN DO IT, YOU CAN DO IT, YOU CAN DO IT!

Fear's Hidden Chemistry

Fear is a phantom that doesn't exist, just an illusion, a chemical reaction that holds you back. The only purpose of fear is to keep us from going where we have great growth, a destiny.

Virus programs, installations, beliefs do not allow you to go there, as by going there, you lose their source of energy. These programs feed on you and take away your opportunities. They make you believe you're stuck. But once you break free, you'll see your true power. The moment you act despite fear, you reclaim control over your life and open doors to endless possibilities.

Your created hero has gained confidence and steps forward through darkness even without expecting something else as he is not even recognized with this world yet. As suddenly on this path, the character is attacked by an 8-foot spider. Your character felt pain his body for the first time since the spider bite into his arm. Your character was getting worse it started to see darkness in his eyes, weakness as he suddenly falls.

Stranger

A stranger gives you an antidote. You drink it, but the weakness remains. Slowly, you open your eyes. The stranger's face is there, but it's unrecognizable, blurred, like a shadow. In the background, the dead spider lies, its lifeless body a sign of the stranger's action to save you.

You *(weakly)*: "Who are you?"
Stranger *(calmly)*: "My name is Friend."
Friend: "You must believe in this, in yourself. The poison... it is deadly, yes. It feels like the devil itself, but remember, its power only exists as much as we give it. Your journey isn't over yet, but only your faith will guide you through this. The antidote will only work if you believe it will."
You *(nods weakly)*: "Thank you, Stranger... by the name of Friend."

LEAF PEOPLE
BRANCH PEOPLE
ROOT PEOPLE

The Tree of Humanity

Leaf People, Branch People, and Root People.

Leaf People: Some individuals in your life are like leaves on a tree. They are there for only a season. You can't rely on them because they are weak and fleeting. Like leaves, they take what they need, and as soon as it gets cold or a strong wind blows, they disappear. It's just who they are, and you can't be angry at them for it.

Branch People: Other people are like branches on a tree. They are stronger than leaves but still need careful consideration. They stick around through most seasons, but during life's storms, they might break. While they are stronger than leaves, you must test them before relying heavily on them. Most can't handle too much pressure. But again, it's just who they are, and there's no point in being mad at them or blaming them.

Root People: If you find people in your life who are like the roots of a tree, you've found something special. Root people are rare because they don't seek attention. Their purpose is to support you and help you live a strong, healthy life. They thrive when you thrive, staying low-key and unseen, but their presence is vital. During the worst storms, they hold you up, nourish you, and provide strength. Just as a tree relies on its roots for growth, take a moment to appreciate the true supporters in your life.

How many leaves, branches, and roots do you have? And what are you in the lives of others?

Thank you God for Your Roots!

"Share this message, uplift others, and create change. Together, we grow. Mention @mylifexsoul in your story!"

Parents Are a Bridge

I would like to touch on a relevant topic and share my philosophical thoughts. Parents are a bridge to the new generation. They connect the past with the future, offering wisdom and values to guide us. But just like a bridge, their role is to help us move forward, not to carry us forever.

What is the mission of parents? Until now, I have come to the opinion that the goal of parents is to leave a new life after themselves, its continuation and growth.

The essence is not to be exactly like your father or your mother. Each parent, whether dominant or of a different personality, is encoded in the child. In short, half of your parents live inside you.

My parents allowed me to observe both their strengths and weaknesses, giving me the opportunity to reflect on their models. From this, I've learned how to understand and work with these qualities, both strengths and weaknesses, to create the life I desire. Because those weaknesses can be encoded in the child, and it is up to the child to decide whether to continue or transform.

Parents are the beginning, like a bridge connecting two distant points. They offer us a view from where they stand, but it's up to us to see beyond that. Our task is not to follow their path exactly, but to learn from it, grow from it, and create our own journey. The real power lies in taking what we've learned and using it to shape a life that's uniquely ours.

The Desire to Teach Parents

It often happens that in teenage years a child wants to teach his parents... The child always thinks he sees and knows better, but you don't have to teach your parents, if they want to improve and work on themselves, they will. Better show them your support, because you probably need support for yourself, too.

The task is to collect information, analyze it and create your own generation. There are times when the child financially supports the parents, and that is nice, but sometimes the result is that the parents completely relax and die inside. Communication is the answer and the way out of illusions.

In general, *"Our Generation"* is about development, from one generation to the next. It's about growth, it's a stairway to the top. Leaving legacy after legacy is development.

Take, for example, the car. From one generation to the next, the car's capabilities and design have changed, it has *"evolved."* Every time a new engineer, designer, developer, etc. came into the world and made it their *"own."*

Let's be grateful and create.

Keep your self-control, the less you react, the better you will be able to handle the situation. Before you say something that you will later regret, take a deep breath and slowly count to 10.

Continuing the Path

Friend *(hands you a sword)*:
"I'm glad you've recovered and found belief in yourself. You're ready to continue your journey."
Friend *(pauses, looking serious)*:
"Take this. You'll need it. Defend yourself, and fight the barriers ahead. It's time for me to go my own way now. If our paths cross again, If our paths cross again, I'll be there. But for now, goodbye."

Gratitude and Faith will heal You!

Unexpected troubles can happen both, in life and in your game character life. Our thoughts are so powerful and influential that if we allow ourselves to be consumed by them, they can lead to self-destruction, causing us to lose touch with who we truly are. Many studies suggest that a large portion of our thoughts tend to be negative, which can influence how we see the world and ourselves.

This is scientifically proven, just imagine what kind of inner dialogue takes place and what kind of energy we charge our body with. Therefore, it is important in different situations, good or bad, to remain grateful and believe that this way you become stronger and smarter.

Holding a grudge or anger only causes illness and attracting similar situations to repeat the lesson.

I believe that we are here to learn, though I don't know what comes next. When I reflect on the bigger picture, I begin to truly understand the purpose of it all. If I were to close my eyes and pass away, it would all disappear. Later, at the end of the book, I'll share my point of view on this. **If fear resides in your subconscious, change can become hard. But I'm here to help you!**

Our thoughts shape our emotional state. Emotions create actions. Actions lead us to a result. People often limit themselves, especially when it comes to success, by their own thoughts and the opinions of others. What if, instead of holding back, we let go of limitations? With love and faith, we take action and let success follow.

2. Mission:

Write on the paper below: What am I grateful for?

Take a moment to reflect. What fills your heart with gratitude today?
What people, moments, or experiences have made a positive impact on your life?
Write them down here. Let this be your reminder of the abundance you already have.

If you're constantly waiting for others to validate your worth, seeking approval through recognition of your success or material achievements, you're unknowingly setting yourself up to depend on the opinions of those around you. Over time, this can lead to feelings of emptiness and inadequacy.

True confidence comes only when you begin to build your self-worth on a deep, internal understanding of who you are and where you're headed, not on the judgments of others. Sooner or later, this mindset will pay off, and you'll stop worrying about what you may lack along the way.

Real attraction and value don't come from external validation. What truly matters is that you're an ambitious, hardworking individual, filled with inner strength and driven by a clear purpose. That alone is magnetic if you accept it within yourself. If you're ready to own who you truly are, it will allow you to build healthier, more honest relationships.

Your strength comes from staying on your path, no matter the obstacles or doubts. When you stop seeking approval from others and simply accept their reactions as the element of water, which reflects everything around it yet remains pure within, you free yourself. Let's smile at the mistakes we've made and the lessons we've learned.

"Share this message, uplift others, and create change.
Together, we grow. Mention @mylifexsoul in your story!"

Breaking Free from the Illusion

People are not your property, they are free. How you engage with others is your choice, and this choice can also change depending on the individual's character, morality, and level of personal growth.

What is yours is only for a certain time, like renting a body that has been given to you. You are given talents and gifts that you should use and perhaps even multiply. Waiting until you are rejected, until the coffin lid closes? I'm not kidding, time's up.

You are the creator of your life. You customize it, change it, and define the people who are in your life, the goals you achieve, what is important to you, and what is *"scary"* or *"stupid."*

Think for yourself what is right, what you imagined, what you saw in the movies, what your parents told you, it's just your beliefs. The question is either you created your life or it was created for you and you just exist thinking that you are making a choice.

Life is a continuous cycle, a space, and an environment given for temporary use and growth. It is a journey of learning, where experience is gained without any rating or judgment. One thing I haven't fully understood yet is whether doing nothing can be considered destiny, or if actively listening to yourself and taking action can also be part of it.

Who would I like to be?

Our body can be said to be paralleled with drugs. Emotions are roughly speaking the reaction of your body to thoughts through chemistry, ferments that get from the brain. The body gets used to receiving a certain chemistry. Now when I try to change my mindset, I develop a different chemistry. But the body is still attached to the old patterns, making the change feel difficult.

This is similar to what happens to an addicted person when withdrawal symptoms begin. The body tries to revert to its usual state, which triggers an emotional swing.

"The truth always acts differently."

— Dariusz Romanovski

"Share this message, uplift others, and create change. Together, we grow. Mention @mylifexsoul in your story!"

YOU CAN DO IT, YOU CAN DO IT, YOU CAN DO IT, YOU CAN DO IT!
YOU CAN DO IT, YOU CAN DO IT, YOU CAN DO IT, YOU CAN DO IT!
YOU CAN DO IT, YOU CAN DO IT, YOU CAN DO IT, YOU CAN DO IT!

5

YOU CAN DO IT, YOU CAN DO IT, YOU CAN DO IT, YOU CAN DO IT!
YOU CAN DO IT, YOU CAN DO IT, YOU CAN DO IT, YOU CAN DO IT!
YOU CAN DO IT, YOU CAN DO IT, YOU CAN DO IT, YOU CAN DO IT!

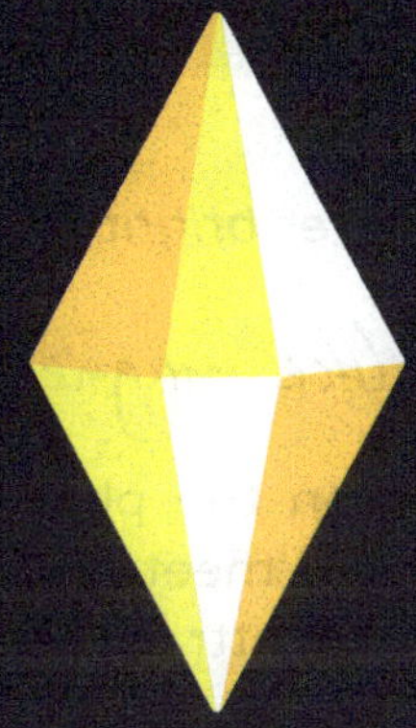

CHAPTER 5:
WE LIKE MAGNETS: WISE MAN

Installing 40%

Have You Ever Played the Sims?

You see a man ahead, like a magnet pulling you toward him. As you get closer, a yellow light starts flashing brightly above his head. You step cautiously toward him.

You: "Hi..."
Mr. Unknown: *(Smiling, his eyes bright with intrigue.)*

Why are we like magnets to others?

There are so many people on the planet, every day we see new people. It can be a one-second meetup or it can last for years. Have you ever wondered why we are attracted to a certain person? Why!?

One day, I was just standing in the city, observing people around me. Each of them had their own direction, but what if that direction could change because of someone they meet?

I have a theory that we only meet people at a certain stage of our lives. I will try to express it in an easy and understandable language. Every day, we make countless decisions, each one creating a path and shaping our personal story. So, our result determines more what kind of people we have met on our life path. Why am I attracted to this person and not to another? My perspective is that, at the soul level, the personality of this person resonates with the energy of my own soul. Why do some unexpected meetings lead to marriage, while others connect you with like-minded people who share your interests?

Let's dive deeper, fear defines, but it doesn't define you. You have the opportunity to approach this person or pass by, but life will go on anyway. One thing you must understand is that you can't bring it back. Time won't wait, so create your life as a creator.

I don't think you're the kind of person who, in old age, wakes up and realizes that this is life, only to regret or live in the past, clinging to their youth for the rest of their days. Instead, right now, you're just a step away from the finish line. No one will remember what you were like or how you ended, but they'll remember if you invested something meaningful in this world or in the lives of others.

Right now, if you're attracted, you can approach this person and understand why you were attracted to him, and not guess. Even if it was a meeting for only 5 minutes and somehow ended on a negative note, it taught you a lot, and do not forget that you crossed your barrier—fear. This does not mean the end, but only the beginning of a great one, as this situation could prepare you more for an important meeting and preparation. Think more widely and gratefully.

Therefore, sometimes we are no longer interested in the past or what we were doing, as our level of soul and personality has grown and is already on other goals and tasks. Sleep and tears are like the end of the old and the beginning of the new, and yes, everything depends on us how at that time we made the decision to grow or stay the same.

I believe that a certain goal possesses an energy force, which means the attraction of certain people to realize this goal, as well as the attraction of the situation to achieve and become the person who master's this goal. If you have already chosen this book and are reading it, then there is something special about you and this is a certain step in your life. **Are you loyal to your desire?**

Why do I give you an opportunity if you don't accept it and play with it. As I said before, your goal or desire is charged with a certain energy and call it manifestation whatever you want, if you show persistence and confidence in your choice, with your confidence and desire, more and more opportunities are being attracted into your life to fulfill that desire.

It could be someone, an experience, an injury or even a setback, anything that stops you and makes you ask if you are doing the right thing in life. No one is trying to punish you here, you are the creator. Sometimes, though, we can't truly see ourselves from the outside. And yes, that's the real beauty of this world. I'm just getting started.

WHEN THE STUDENT IS READY, THE TEACHER COMES IN.

We often think of the people we meet as simply part of the journey, but what if each person who crosses your path has a deeper purpose? Whether they bring joy, challenges, or lessons, every encounter holds the potential to shape your growth and transform your life. Some people may appear for just a moment, while others stay by your side for years, yet all contribute in meaningful ways.

In this section, we'll explore the six profound purposes that people serve in your life, helping you understand how each relationship plays a crucial role in your personal evolution. Ready to discover how the people in your life are guiding you toward becoming the best version of yourself?

The Six Purposes of People in Your Life:

To Teach You a Lesson: People enter our lives to teach us valuable lessons we might not have learned otherwise. Often, these lessons come with pain, leaving us feeling broken or unhappy. Yet, it is through these tough times that we gain wisdom and strength. Disappointments and difficulties often teach us more than success ever could. Life will continue to present similar challenges and obstacles until we truly learn the lesson it has for us. If you find yourself repeatedly encountering the same situations, consider the lessons these individuals bring.

To Help You See Yourself from a New Angle: Some people help us see ourselves in a different light, opening our eyes to things we might not notice on our own. Sometimes we get so caught in routines that we fail to see the impact of our actions. Then, someone arrives who reflects our strengths and abilities, reigniting our confidence and motivation. Conversely, others might reflect our flaws, urging us to address what holds us back. This process, though difficult, is necessary for growth. No matter the outcome, you will never be the same after meeting such individuals.

To Provide Support During Tough Times: Certain people come into our lives when we need support the most. Whether it's offering a shoulder to cry on, lending a listening ear, or providing practical help, these people are a lifeline during times of adversity. Their presence helps us build resilience and navigate through life's challenges with more strength and less loneliness.

To Challenge and Push You Forward: Some individuals push us out of our comfort zones, encouraging us to reach for more. They see our potential and won't let us settle for less. Through their influence, we grow, rise to new heights, and accomplish more than we thought possible.

To Share Joy and Celebrate Success: Life is full of joyful moments, and certain special people are there to share them with you. These individuals bring happiness, celebrate your victories, and fill your life with positivity. They remind us of the importance of cherishing good times and enjoying life's blessings.

To Fulfill a Mutual Purpose or Goal: Some people enter your life because you share a common goal or purpose. Whether in personal or professional pursuits, collaborating with these individuals can lead to shared success and lasting bonds. Their presence helps you achieve something significant together, strengthening mutual respect and creating lasting connections.

Ultimately, every person who comes into your life has a purpose. They are there to teach you something, to help you grow, or to guide you along your journey. At every turn, whether their impact is uplifting or challenging, every encounter is an opportunity to gain insight, build resilience, and move closer to your true potential.

So embrace the connections you make, reflect on the lessons they bring, and let them shape you into the best version of yourself. Remember, no meeting is accidental. Every individual you meet is part of the masterpiece that is your life.

No one else defines my destiny, my strength, the fire within me, or my happiness. Learn, grow, forgive, be grateful, and keep moving forward with purpose and an open heart, knowing that each step brings you closer to the person you're meant to become.

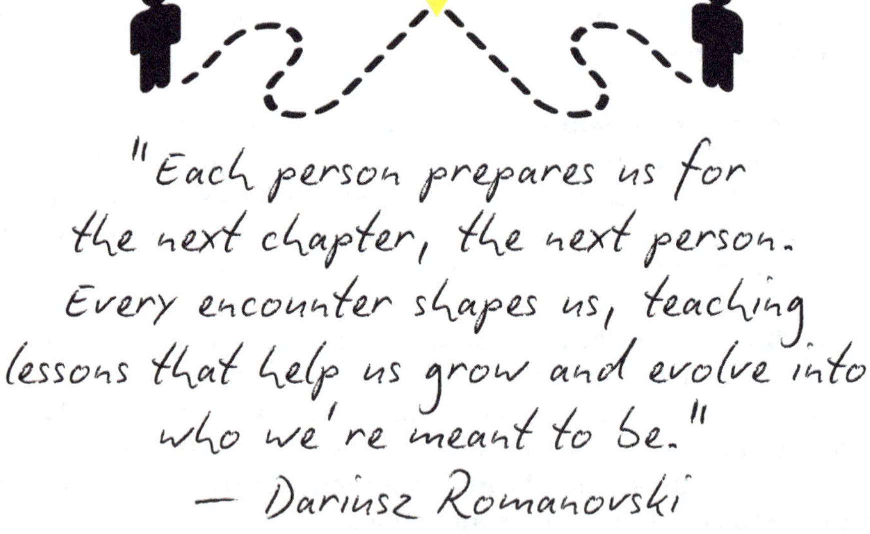

"Share this message, uplift others, and create change.
Together, we grow. Mention @mylifexsoul in your story!"

A Journey to New Horizons

Lessons from the Old Wise Man

Wise Man: "Hello, my dear friend!"
You: "Where am I?"

Wise Man: "You're in a world of opportunities."

As he speaks, a shadowy figure with a scythe suddenly attacks the old man. Without hesitation, you rush forward and strike at the shadowy presence with the sword the "Friend" gave you, shouting, "I am grateful for this man—leave him alone!" In an instant, the attacker disappears.

Wise Man *(he hands you something)*:
"Thank you... I am the last Light of Wisdom in this world."
You: "The Light of Wisdom?"
Wise Man: "Take this. It's for you."
You: "What is it?"
Wise Man: "It's money."
"You can't buy time, and you can't get it back... but you've gifted me some more time."
You: "Why do I need this?"
Wise Man: "This is money. It is the currency of value, trust, gratitude, and exchange. You can buy anything with it... except time and health. I'll explain more later."

You: "Where am I from?"
Wise Man: "Ah, so you're a new soul... Your soul grows with your experience. You're lucky to have me as your mentor. I suppose you came from this forest. But now your mind will begin to see more. This world is bigger than you think."
You: "What... What do you mean?"
Wise Man: "Ah, yes, you will meet the Dragon of Wishes."
You: "A Dragon!? What! What do you mean?!"
Wise Man: "Ha, ha! I believe you are the chosen one. You will definitely see him."
You: "But... how can I see him?"

Wise Man: "It's a journey of a thousand miles. Right now, your mind can only see the width of what you've experienced, but once I share this knowledge with you, your horizons will expand. Come, let me take you to my house. I'll explain it to you. It might be difficult to understand with your present point of view, but I'll help you see the bigger picture."

The Wise man grabs a stick and starts drawing on the ground, explaining to you.

If your inner voice is asking, "How?" it's a sign you're stepping beyond your comfort zone. Remind yourself, "I'm learning, I'm growing, and I have the strength to make it happen!

The Wise Mind's Expanded Horizon

The Horizon of Your
Character's Mindset

How can I expand my horizon of thinking? You must move forward, but not just move, but also with your mindset. Right now, you're looking for the Dragon of Wishes, and as an example, **he's here.**

The Unseen Path

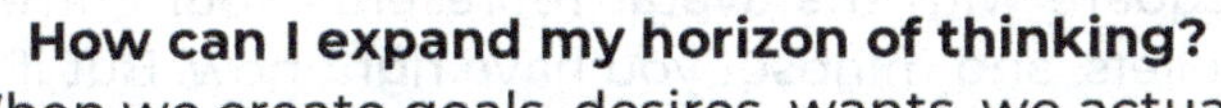

How can I expand my horizon of thinking?

When we create goals, desires, wants, we actually expand our subconscious (BLUE) mind and the horizon of thinking. It's as if we're planting a seed in that area. We're like the lions who conquer territory, expand borders, but only in the subconscious, in the mentality.

Horizon Stories

The green square with the avatar represents your current self, the thoughts, beliefs, and mindset you have right now. But if you decide you want to improve your life, for example, by becoming more confident, your horizon of thinking starts to expand. You might realize that in order to be more confident, you need to change how you view yourself and the world around you. Perhaps you start practicing positive affirmations, challenging limiting beliefs, or stepping outside your comfort zone.

With every goal, your mindset grows, and the actions you take become more aligned with the person you want to become. It's not just about wishing for change. It's about expanding your horizon of thinking and taking steps toward becoming your best self, and realizing that it is possible.

The question is, what is your thinking horizon right now? The current horizon is a world in which there are certain people, your environment, which may not even support your life choices. They think they know what is best for you. Answer, have you ever talked about your desires or goals and been called a dreamer or made fun of for it?

When you expand your horizons of thinking, be prepared to let go of the old and your familiar surroundings. Clinging to them no longer serves you and isn't worth the effort.

Sometimes, growth and choosing your path aren't about holding on to things that never tried to hold you back. It's about letting go to make space for something new. That path may be lonely, but be grateful for where you're headed, and trust yourself.

For those who are open, there is God. I am sure there will be people in the new horizons you reach, waiting for you, ready to appreciate and believe in the life you are creating.

I believe in you and the life you're creating. I believe in your ability to reach your goals, fulfill your desires, and turn your dreams into reality!

Too much energy is wasted making excuses about why we can't be, do, or have what we want. Imagine how much you could achieve if you just stopped talking and put that energy to work.

Often when we say that we don't have the skills for something, what we are really saying is that we are too scared to try, not what we are really not good at. It is usually not lack of experience that holds us back, but lack of commitment to do what it takes to succeed.

Claiming Your Potential

Affirmations, meditations, visualizations, the sum of all the actions that help to put the whole puzzle together, it is not something magical. This is a way of talking to yourself.

Thoughts don't materialize in a way that you think money is going to fall on you or that it is going to fall from the sky. The point is that you create the opportunities and enable yourself to have more, living a better life.

If we look at nature and philosophy, we see that we are like lions that claim territory, expand borders, but it is all in the subconscious, in the mind. Our wishes expand the limits of our subconscious. The pattern of my world and your consciousness remains the same, but when we start allowing ourselves new horizons in this world, when we start realizing that I can / want to do more.

I begin to believe that I can live better.

Create a new horizon for yourself.

Menu

"LIFE IS LIKE A BUFFET.

SOME PEOPLE CAN TAKE AS MUCH AS THEY WANT.

SOME PEOPLE TAKE AS MUCH AS THEIR CONSCIENCE ALLOWS THEM,

AND SOME PEOPLE HAVE THE IMPUDENCE TO TAKE AS MUCH AS THEY WANT.

BUT THE SAME RULE APPLIES TO EVERYONE.

YOU CAN'T TAKE ANYTHING WITH YOU."

WOULD YOU LIKE TO ORDER SOMETHING ELSE?

— DARIUSZ ROMANOVSKI

"Share this message, uplift others, and create change. Together, we grow. Mention @mylifexsoul in your story!"

YOU CAN DO IT, YOU CAN DO IT, YOU CAN DO IT, YOU CAN DO IT!
YOU CAN DO IT, YOU CAN DO IT, YOU CAN DO IT, YOU CAN DO IT!
YOU CAN DO IT, YOU CAN DO IT, YOU CAN DO IT, YOU CAN DO IT!

YOU CAN DO IT, YOU CAN DO IT, YOU CAN DO IT, YOU CAN DO IT!
YOU CAN DO IT, YOU CAN DO IT, YOU CAN DO IT, YOU CAN DO IT!
YOU CAN DO IT, YOU CAN DO IT, YOU CAN DO IT, YOU CAN DO IT!

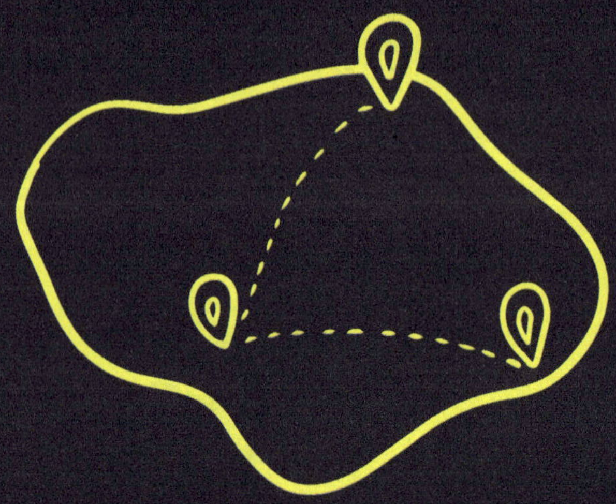

CHAPTER 6:
WHERE THE HEART POINTS

Installing 50%

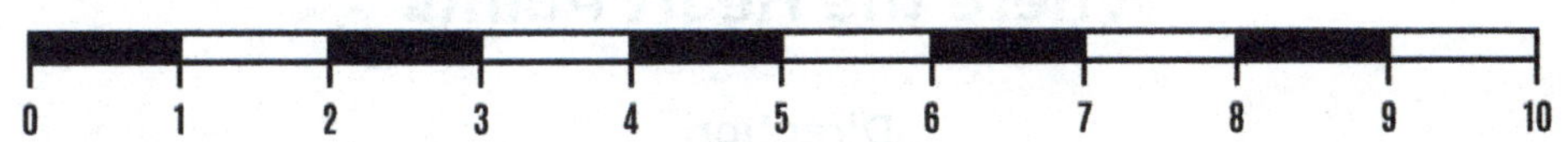

"Let your heart guide you, because it knows the way when the mind is lost.."

— Unknown

"Share this message, uplift others, and create change. Together, we grow. Mention @mylifexsoul in your story!"

Where the Heart Points

Direction

You *(confused)*: "Where am I supposed to go?"
Wise man: "Depending on where you want to arrive. Let me tell you a parable about Oasis."

Parable

We are working hard, but we are not getting any closer to a result, the thing is that we are trying to make the ants do the work of the Elephant!

The story begins with an introduction to the ant.
He is very unhappy, always working, never earning enough, and barely making ends meet. I think you get the idea.

Typical life of an ant, isn't it? But the ant is constantly haunted by the feeling that somewhere out there is a much more interesting and richer life, one that he was born for but which he can't reach.

(An owl appears.)
***(The Old Wise Owl hears the cries of an ant about his life)*:**
"Hi, buddy! You look a bit upset."
Ant: "Yes! I'm really upset. I work hard all the time. I barely make ends meet, but I feel I was born for something more."
Owl: "Because you were born for more! And imagine that you can achieve all this and get everything you want, but first you must get to the Oasis."
Ant: "Oasis? I thought it was just a fairy tale, does it really exist?"
Owl: "It does exist. And you need to get there. But what's even better: you can get there, it's not that far. The oasis is strictly east from here."
Ant: "Great! How do I get there? Can we go now?"
Owl: "You see, there's a problem here, Ant. You can't see it, of course, but you live on the back of an elephant. And this elephant is currently going west. You can go-go... as long as you like, but until the elephant you live on turns around, you won't get there."

Discover the language with the elephant. Your subconscious mind the huge elephant that is responsible for forward movement thinks only in visual ways. Unlike the conscious mind, which uses words, thoughts and logical connections, the subconscious mind is entirely visual and emotional.

In fact, this is the best way to understand what the subconscious mind does. The subconscious elephant within you simply sees a target (a clear image) and moves in that direction. This can only be achieved by letting go of the situation and immersing yourself in intuition, flair, and creativity.

"Slow down to speed up."

Just before a performance, the best athletes don't just slow down. They stop completely and concentrate to create an accurate mental picture of the desired result. They visualize it then the subconscious mind makes it real.

YOU CAN DO IT, YOU CAN DO IT, YOU CAN DO IT, YOU CAN DO IT!
YOU CAN DO IT, YOU CAN DO IT, YOU CAN DO IT, YOU CAN DO IT!
YOU CAN DO IT, YOU CAN DO IT, YOU CAN DO IT, YOU CAN DO IT!

7

YOU CAN DO IT, YOU CAN DO IT, YOU CAN DO IT, YOU CAN DO IT!
YOU CAN DO IT, YOU CAN DO IT, YOU CAN DO IT, YOU CAN DO IT!
YOU CAN DO IT, YOU CAN DO IT, YOU CAN DO IT, YOU CAN DO IT!

CHAPTER 7.1: BETTING SECONDS: THE BILLIONAIRE GAME

Installing 55%

How Money Shapes Your Reality

It costs nothing to treat anyone with respect. Making money isn't just about the money itself, just like losing weight isn't just about the weight, and finding a soulmate isn't just about the soulmate. It's about who you become and what you believe is possible for you.

The Wise Man and His Knowledge About Money

You: "Wise man, what is it, and why do I even need it?"
Wise man: "Money is just a tool, like everything else."
(He gestures broadly to the horizon, as if painting a picture of possibilities.)
Wise man: "But if you change your point of view, you'll see it's about more than survival. It's about contributing to a better world."

Wise man *(he looks you in the eye, his tone steady)*:
"Having money comes with responsibility. The more you have, the more you're called to share. To truly make a difference, you must be rich in every sense: psychologically, spiritually, energetically, and materially. Remember that the best way to improve the world is to first improve yourself."

There is a big difference between telling everybody how you want to make a million a year and having a clear, and determined plan. Money alone means nothing.

It is our appreciation of money that gives it meaning and inspires us to have money in our lives. Some people have a negative view of money because of their childhood or their environment. Money is a neutral energy, a belief that either attracts or distances us from it. The more value I bring to the world, the more opportunities will come my way, including financial rewards, but it's not just about the money. Or from a different perspective, money is evil. My parents lived in debt and believed it was all the fault of money.

Until you change the way you think, money won't change anything. Money is everywhere, surrounded by opportunities. Don't focus on earning money, but on committing to create. **What can you create out of love?**

Do you know what money truly does for you, or is it the feeling it gives you? The only thing that evokes feelings is the image of you spending that money and seeing yourself in that scenario.

The subconscious mind is like a little child that sees only itself and is driven by the images it creates. Money is good, but it's never the main thing. It's all about the process, how you achieve and how you improve. Overcoming yourself, your laziness, your weaknesses, and choosing the right path for your soul. It may not be easy, but it's the right choice for growth and fulfillment.

It’s often said that achieving success starts with investing in yourself. Committing a small percentage of your desired income to personal growth can make all the difference. Whether you reach your goals depends on your choice.

Dear Reader,

let’s go deeper, as the answers are hidden within. You don’t need to think too hard right now. Yes, critical thinking has its place, but for now, let the flow of information guide you toward clarity.

Don't chase money, chase your dreams and the vision of what you want to do in this world.

WHAT COMES BEFORE MONEY?

"Money is not just currency, it is the energy that flows through the veins of our ambitions, shaping the world we create."
— Dariusz Romanovski

MONEY

To make money, it's not just about the money. Just like losing weight isn't only about the number on the scale, and finding a soulmate isn't just about the person. It's about who you become and what you believe is possible for you.

You're not the only one who dreams of wealth or achieving big goals. But the real reason many don't succeed is that they fail to realize one simple truth. Time is the most valuable currency.

Everything you create and everything you learn to manage lays the foundation for greater opportunities to come. Too often, we focus on what we lack and fall into depression. Instead, shift your focus to your strengths and ask yourself:

What can I create with what I already have?

Let's take money as an example. If you can't manage the resources you currently have or use them to create what you desire, what will happen when greater wealth enters your life? Will you be ready for it, or might it overwhelm you? Now, think about time. Are you managing it wisely enough to achieve your dreams?

Let me share a fresh viewpoint with you, a personal philosophy that could change the way you see the time you have.

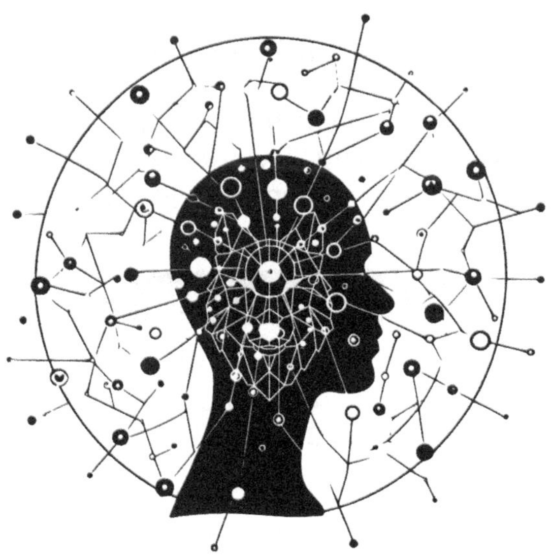

Time: The Greatest Currency

Now, imagine this: You enter life as a wealthy billionaire, at least in time. For instance, **70 years equals 2,207,520,000 seconds.**

Achieving your dream goals requires your attention and your seconds. For example, a dream car costs someone 10,000,000 seconds or even 150,000,000 seconds, and these seconds are deducted from your balance. **There is a guardian angel who acts as a personal accountant and assistant, understanding our wants and needs.** This guardian not only protects, helps, and sends signals, but also uses our seconds ***(currency)*** properly.

The question is, do we truly listen to our guardian angel?

For example, here's how earning $1 billion in 10 years or $1 million in 5 years could look when broken down into smaller units. Money is not a goal, and I'll tell you why later.

$1 Billion in 10 Years:

- **10 Years =** 120 months, **1 Month =** $8,333,333
- **1 Day =** $378,787 (assuming 22 workdays/month)
- **1 Hour =** $17,217 (assuming 8 hours/day)
- **1 Second** ≈ $0.48

$1 Million in 5 Years:

- **5 Years =** 60 months, **1 Month =** $16,667
- **1 Day =** $757.09 (assuming 22 workdays/month)
- **1 Hour =** $94.64 (assuming 8 hours/day)
- **1 Second** ≈ $0.0263

Understand this. Every level teaches you something new. At each level, you're not just growing financially, you're growing in wisdom.

At $1,000, you build discipline and skill. At $10,000, you master strategy. By the time you hit $100,000, your focus expands to thinking in bigger terms: scalability, systems, and impact.

The amount chosen is a symbol of self-belief, and the path to it is the true result. Start with $20,000. It may seem like a solid goal, but at this level, your thinking can be limited. You're often focused on working for someone else, taking on smaller projects, or relying on short-term goals.

Now, aim higher. Picture $200,000. This requires a different way of thinking. It calls for a strategic mindset, one that views money not as the end goal but as the result of creating something much more powerful: a business, systems, and value that can scale. You learn to monetize your talents in new, innovative ways. Now you understand that $200,000 isn't just about earning. It's about becoming someone who creates opportunities and makes a bigger impact.

People who own multi-million-dollar homes didn't start by simply dreaming about those homes. In fact, they were once just like you, with humble ambitions and a vision that seemed far out of reach. They didn't focus on luxury or status, instead, they focused on what they could create, the systems, the projects, the solutions that would transform industries and change lives.

Nobody starts by aiming for a $55 million house. When you start, those numbers seem beyond imagination.

At first, you set achievable goals, and once you've earned your first million, your horizons expand. They didn't begin by thinking about buying things, but by building things that mattered.

The money, the houses, the fame, those came later as a side effect and natural result of their focus on creating value or being the best in their chosen field. They set goals that challenged them, grew them, and pushed them to become more than they were. It's a process, not something that happens overnight.

Aiming for $1 billion from a healthy perspective is about more than just a number. It's a reflection of high ambition. It's about becoming the person who can create lasting value, lead effectively, and think strategically. **Grow gradually but confidently.**

It's better to take one step at a time rather than trying to jump to the 10th step. While you're overthinking, old age might arrive and you may not be able to jump at all. Take baby steps, and the key is to keep moving forward.

In today's world, money is akin to the skill of a hunter. In the Stone Age, a man was valued for his ability to hunt, securing stability and the well-being of future generations. His knowledge was shared, ensuring survival. At the same time, women played distinct roles within the family. These ancient instincts still persist today. This drive for growth is simply part of the journey.

There are many ways to make money, depending on your chosen role in life and your degree of morality. One fact remains: money is printed and flows like energy.

So, who makes money—the producer or the consumer? It's one thing to think that producing and selling makes money. It's another to live under the illusion that a consumer in a producer's system can earn without investing in themselves.

Let's dive into the world of casinos, which I found personally interesting to study. They say it's a form of entertainment, but it's also a business. What kind of business is it?

Let's pretend we're a casino.
Now, answer this: how would I lure you to my place?
How about showing friendship and showing that we care? What if we offer you a free drink? Or a free spin game with my virtual money? Feeling lucky?

CONSUMER OR PRODUCER?
WHAT'S YOUR ROLE?

As soon as you entertain the thought, it turns into an emotion and action, and at that point, you've already lost before you even start. A drink of alcohol reduces your level of critical thinking, which benefits someone else.

If you're a highly emotional person, you will likely lose. This is where things get interesting by understanding how the human brain works psychologically. If I won once or twice, why not invest my money to increase my winnings? It's not the casino's money or virtual currency, it's your money. And win again? Yes!

The moment you see your real money doubled, you might think, *"Maybe this could be my job?"* If you allow yourself such thoughts, you become a slave. The next thing you realize is that you're losing.

Then you start thinking maybe it's because you've invested too little or too much. In addition, you're treated to free alcohol, creating an artificial bubble where all you think about is gambling and the desire to get rich through casino games. In the heart of the casino, you're spending your own money, oblivious to the passing time, as the absence of windows keeps you in a world where reality fades.

But why? Because of gambling. *"WHAT IF?"* You get lucky once, and you believe you'll get lucky again. Or you'll try again, intuitively believing in it. If you add spirituality, gods, and angels into it, you become a hostage. You've lost some of your money, and the casino offers you a free night's stay at a hotel, understanding your situation. You feel taken care of, but once you sober up and regain clarity, you'll either realize in the morning that some of your money is gone, or your family will be unpleasantly surprised.

What if this person is now facing the consequences of his actions? Maybe he'll regain some common sense, but he allowed himself to believe this could be his primary source of income. Why work hard or worry when you can turn $20 into $100 in less than two minutes? Why? Because you got lucky?

"No one who drowned in the water ever thought they would."

It's Showtime!

And now it's showtime. I repeat, thoughts turn into actions. In the chaos of it all, there's the thought of winning, denying the reality that he lost everything. And what can a human truly want inside when everyone around him is angry?

I will prove them wrong, solve my problems, and take care of my parents. I imagine a picture where the sun is shining, a happy family is together, money flows freely, and we live in a luxurious house with everyone smiling, including me.

In this image, with pride and confidence, feeling like a god and believing he's capable of beating the casino, he takes out a loan and may even risk his house, betting everything on black. He loses.

Alternatively, he wins but doesn't withdraw. Instead, he continues playing, hoping to double his winnings, only to eventually lose everything.

Remember, I told you that when a newborn enters the world, they're a billionaire, 2,207,520,000 seconds. So, all thoughts and visions are shattered, and there's no turning back time. The bet has been made. Against this background, children may see their parents fighting about money or watching their father being almost destroyed and creating the belief that money is evil.

Don't Wait for Luck—Create Your Own Path!

Behind the pursuit of realizing your dream life, there are many paths and just as many consequences. You probably recognize this feeling. "By the time I'm 20, 25, or 30, I will be a millionaire or achieve my dream life." The truth is, you're not the only one who thinks that way. But the most important thing is to realize, not just imagine or wish.

Saying "I'm still young, everything is in the future" doesn't get you any closer to that picture. The more you wait for something, the further away it gets.

What's the difference between you and a gambler who thinks he'll get lucky next time? Doing the same actions and expecting better results is foolish.

So, which path will you choose? The best investment is in yourself. If you fail or lose something, the knowledge, skills, and abilities will remain, ready to be polished like a diamond and tried again. Or you can bet everything on black and end up without even the power of spirit. Everything happens between people, with God's guidance and the direction of the Universe. You're not here to simply play by someone else's rules, but to fulfill your own purpose in harmony with a greater plan.

With a clear understanding of your values, desires, ideas, and priorities, you can shape your life with intention and purpose. It's a playground for lessons and personal development. When you're primarily a consumer, you're exploring the world and enjoying its creations. But to unlock your fullest potential, you must also step into the role of a creator, building your own path while learning from and adding to what others have already created.

What comes before money?

When setting goals, think about the deeper impact you want to make. For example, you could set a goal of earning $10,000 through your side business, or you could focus on how many lives you want to improve through your service or product. Which one fuels your passion more, financial gain or the sense of fulfillment from knowing you've helped others?

True motivation often comes from a deeper purpose. When your goals align with that purpose, creativity flows naturally, and the path to achieving them becomes clearer.

The path to this goal is an adventure and the most valuable, which allows you to grow. I don't think you were told to be born to come to this earth to make $1,000,000, and that's it.

Let's take the next step, because waiting for things to happen won't get us any closer to our dreams!

YES! **YES!** **YES!**

From Wishes to Action

The strongest person can give up, the most talented person can give up, and the loneliest person can give up. It's the easiest choice—to give up. But life isn't about waiting for the storm to pass. It's about learning to dance in the rain. This reminds us to find strength and meaning in tough times rather than giving up.

You have the Opportunity!

As long as you're alive, you have the ***"OPPORTUNITY."*** Fall in love with these words, feel it, but I respect a person's personal choice. If you chose the path of high ambition, entrepreneurship, is this about the lonely path?

You are a motivator for yourself and for others, you are the captain of the ship, you.. I can continue, but I want to note that this is a gift and an opportunity to develop yourself as a person even more. Everyone will achieve exactly as much as they need.

Do you want to be weird? And it doesn't scare you or make you uncomfortable. But if you want to give up, take a moment to reflect and pay attention to yourself, asking the important question, *"Who am I?"* By understanding your true self, desires, and purpose, you can shape the life you truly want, rather than the one others try to dictate. Every person is unique and valuable. Each individual is worth noting, and most importantly, everyones environment is shaped by their experiences, values, and the choices they make along the way.

Suicide is not an option. It is a farewell to everything that is inside you. What dream, idea, and goal will die with you? The sun comes after the tornado. It's a matter of time. Choosing to keep going may, in the end, fill you with gratitude for not making that choice. I've experienced this myself, and I can look back on those moments with a smile. If I'd made that decision, I wouldn't have written this book. But this made me stronger.

Space for Your thoughts:

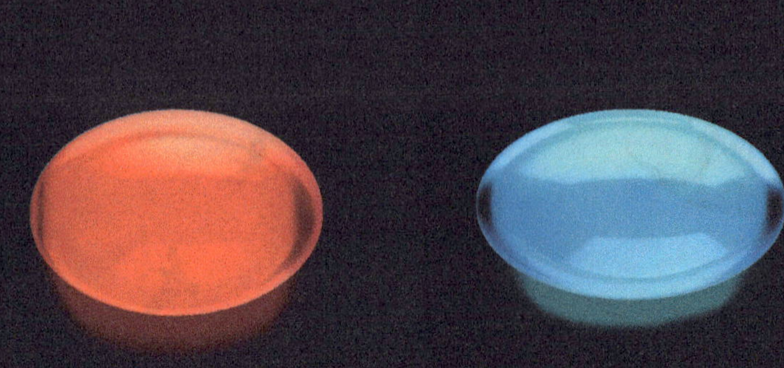

CHAPTER 7.2:

THE KEY TO YOUR NEXT LEVEL

Installing 60%

Red or Blue Pill?

Life is filled with choices, but not all are equal. Some are simple, and their consequences are often clear. These decisions might affect the day, but they rarely change the overall course of our lives. Then there are those rare moments, the ones that define who we are and who we become.

The choice between the *"Red Pill"* and the *"Blue Pill"* is one of those moments. It's the choice that changes everything about how you see yourself and the world around you.

"Blue Pill" is for those who seek safety, comfort, and predictability. It's for those who want to stay in their familiar world, where the rules are known and the risks are low.

"Blue Pill" promises stability an illusion of control. With it, you can go on living your life as you always have, avoiding the pain of uncertainty and the discomfort of change. You keep your head down, follow the rules, and survive, rather than live.

Have we been born to avoid life, or to truly experience it?

But *"Red Pill"* is choice that has the potential to shatter your reality, forces you to confront the truth. It's not for the faint of heart.

"Red Pill" opens your eyes to the world as it truly is, no longer hidden behind a curtain of comforting lies. It's a path to personal growth, but it requires you to leave the familiar behind. It forces you to ask the hard questions. It invites you to grow, to take risks, to face the discomfort of change, and to finally discover your true potential.

Taking the *"Red Pill"* isn't just a moment of clarity or something magical. It's a commitment to yourself, to your future, to the person you have yet to become. You stop waiting for change to happen, and you start making it happen. Stop living on autopilot, and you begin living intentionally. You stop following the crowd, and you create your own path.

But here's the catch: taking *"Red Pill"* is not a one-time decision. It's not about one big moment where you choose to ***"wake up"*** and think you have it all figured out. The red pill choice happens every day. Every time you're faced with fear, with doubt, or with the option to take the easy route, you'll face it again. What, then, is the real question? It's not about which pill you'll choose once, it's about which path you'll choose every single day!

- ***"Red Pill"*** will make you uncomfortable. It will push you to grow, to learn, and to transform. But it will never leave you the same.

- ***"Blue Pill"*** will give you comfort. It will allow you to float through life, safe and unchallenged. But at what cost?

The choice is yours. Always has been!

Professions come and *"die"* every day. Businesses are built and destroyed. Empires bloom and fade.

People, money, and power come and go, but you remain constant. No one can take away your knowledge, your skills, or your way of thinking. Taking *"Red Pill"* means choosing to focus on what truly matters the things that stay with you, the things that you can control. In a world of constant change, **it's your *"POWER,"*** your mind, and your growth that will always define your path.

The Creator-Consumer Balance

As a creator, I've discovered the incredible joy and energy that come from the act of creation itself. It's a state of flow where ideas turn into reality, and passion drives every step.

Interestingly, in a conversation with a consumer, I discovered something profound. Their fulfillment comes not from creating, but from experiencing what's been created. They enjoy the moment of use, the connection to the finished product. This taught me an essential truth. Neither side can exist without the other.

The balance between the creator's joy in the process and the consumer's joy in the result is what brings true harmony to our shared journey.

Unlocking Your Unique Purpose

I believe that every person in the world has a special purpose, a unique place, and a role in this world. There is a concept in Japanese philosophy called Ikigai, which is, roughly speaking, your reason for getting up in the morning. The perfect combination is when you've found a cause that:

1) You love.
2) You are good at.
3) That you can make money from.
4) What is of value, useful to the world.

Many people mistakenly believe that Ikigai is a point in the center that you find, and then everything goes uphill: income, happiness, and meaning. But it doesn't work that way.

Each person is unique and chooses the role they want to live and perform in this life. It is possible to be chosen in any role. There are no limits. Inside you is also a unique soul that feels what is yours and what is not.

Let me help you by asking questions that will allow you to hear yourself if you feel lost. It's quite an interesting game. You can choose to search for yourself or create yourself.

1) What are you proud of?
2) What were your hobbies?
3) What makes you curious?
4) What do you like to learn?
5) What do you do in your free time?
6) What makes you want to do something?
7) What kind of praise do you receive most often?

Ikigai (生き甲斐, lit. a reason for being) is a Japanese concept referring to something that gives a person a sense of purpose, a reason for living.

You have the power to create your own purpose. The key is to look inside, ask the right questions, and take inspired action. Your Ikigai is unique to you. Find it, nurture it, and let it guide you to a life filled with meaning, fulfillment, and joy.

"Share this message, uplift others, and create change. Together, we grow. Mention @mylifexsoul in your story!"

Wealth Through Solutions

Remember, I've shown you ***(on page 94)*** how much you would need to earn to reach $1 billion in 10 years. But what does that really tell you? It might spark an emotional reaction, maybe a sense of financial growth, but it's not the full picture. After all, numbers alone don't create meaning or purpose. However, they are a useful tool for measuring progress.

What are people saying they don't like?
What are people saying they wish existed?
What are people saying that frustrates them?

Someone once said, **"If you want to be a millionaire, solve existing problems. If you want to be a billionaire, create a movement or innovation that transforms the world."** But what does that mean?

Movement & Innovation: A movement is about creating a new way of thinking, a shift in mindset that inspires large groups of people to act or think differently. Think of companies like Apple, which didn't just sell products. They transformed technology into a cultural movement.

Space exploration shows us what's possible when we dare to dream beyond limits. If humanity can build the future among the stars, imagine what you can build in your own life when you refuse to be held back by fear or doubt. Amazon is another one. It didn't just revolutionize shopping. It reshaped the entire retail landscape, including books, by creating a platform that made self-publishing possible and accessible to millions of authors. Amazon redefined how books are sold and read, giving rise to a new generation of writers and readers worldwide.

Religion: On a larger scale, creating a belief system that attracts followers can shape the world in powerful ways. Companies like McDonald's and Nike aren't just selling food or shoes. They've created a *"cult-like"* following, where their values and mission align with their customers lifestyles and beliefs. This creates deep, lasting loyalty that goes beyond simple consumerism.

Airbnb didn't just solve the problem of expensive hotels. They redefined travel by creating a global network of people who share their homes, creating a whole new way of experiencing the world.

Creating a movement or innovation means inspiring people to believe in something bigger than themselves, whether it's through groundbreaking ideas, technological advancements, lifestyle shifts, or cultural trends that reshape how people see and interact with the world.

You should be looking for problems and solutions to those problems, and once you find a solution, build a business around it. Listen to what is happening in the market around you, what people are talking about, and be creative.

STOP chasing money.
CHASE problems.
FIND solutions to those problems.

- People pay you money if they don't know how to do it.
- If what you offer them saves them time and money.
- People pay you when your offering attracts their desire.
- If they can't find something better than what you offer.

The true *"impact"* lies in positively affecting the lives of others, whether it's a few or many.

Everyone defines success in their own way. The person who does the most good is successful in their own way. The person who achieves financial success is successful in their own way. Each person has a unique role in life.

Remember, millionaires and billionaires may share advice, but taking action is up to you. Each person's journey and advice are unique to their market development stages. What used to be a challenge finding unique items is now lost in a sea of options, with price often being the deciding factor. As a result, consumers can easily feel overwhelmed.

True influence doesn't come from being perfect or always flawless. It comes from showing up, contributing authentically, and leaving the world a little better than you found it.

When you positively influence even one person, you manage to start a ripple that can touch countless lives. That's the beauty of influence: it's limitless, expansive, and deeply human.

People don't just buy products, they buy stories, ideas, solutions, desires, and a sense of identity.

Branding is everything. The power of a brand is that it doesn't just sell a product it sells a belief system. This is where companies like Nike, Apple, and Coca-Cola come in. They don't just sell shoes, phones, or cars, they sell a vision of who you are when you use their products.

Billionaires know this. They understand that a product is just a vehicle for a bigger idea or feeling. Your brand must inspire people to feel a connection to it. People are far more willing to spend on something that aligns with their identity, and that's the secret of billionaire brands. They don't just appeal to your needs, they appeal to your soul.

3. Mission:

Business Idea: Identify 10 things that annoy you or that you dislike.

Also check this: Idea Validator
https://founderpal.ai/idea-validator
Get honest feedback on your business idea and build something people truly want.

HEART

Level up

Never stop

I can do it!

PRODUCT
PROBLEM!
DESIRE
ADVERTISEMENT

MONEYLOGY

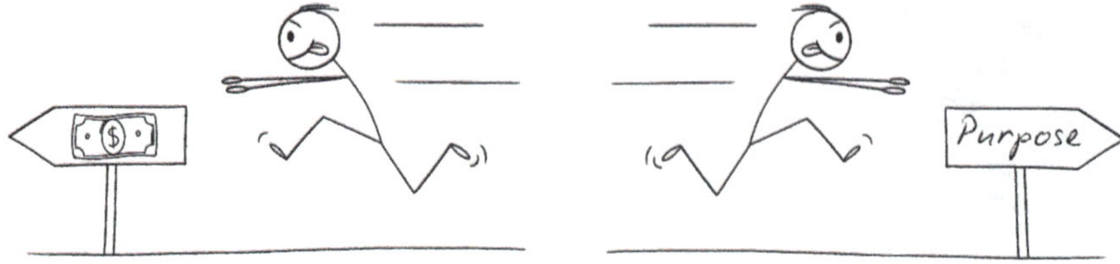

"Purpose or payment? Both have power, but only ideas that touch a need will find true value. To create is to connect." — Dariusz Romanovski

The core of any successful offer is its ability to create real value, solve a problem, or meet a significant need for the target audience.

"Share this message, uplift others, and create change. Together, we grow. Mention @mylifexsoul in your story!"

The Psychology of Money

It's essential to feel that you're genuinely creating value for others. Without a sense of purpose, work can quickly become boring and unmotivating.

WHAT PRODUCT I CAN SELL? - NO!
START ASKING WHAT PROBLEM I CAN SOLVE? It encourages you to focus on the needs and challenges of your audience first.

Problem: Many people feel unmotivated or scared by big tasks, making it hard for them to plan and stay focused, which leads to procrastination and a lack of progress.
Solution: Offer an app that helps users break down big tasks into smaller, more manageable steps, and tracks their progress.

Product Idea: Task Breaker App.
An app that helps users break down large, overwhelming projects into smaller, more achievable tasks. The app could send reminders for each step, offer motivational messages, and track progress in real-time. It could also include a rewards system, where users earn points or badges for completing tasks, keeping them motivated and helping them feel a sense of accomplishment as they move toward their larger goals.

To succeed, solve problems. Whether it's a solution to a serious problem or helping millions of people, the value you create leads to wealth. It's even better when you solve your personal problem, because it can also become your business idea.

For the next week, every time you spend money, even if it's just $1, ask yourself, why did I choose to spend it here? What drew me in? Then consider, what could they have done to make me spend even more? To master how money flows, understanding your spending habits is the first step.

Once you understand this, shift your attention to creating value. **What can you offer that people would willingly exchange their money for? What, even, would attract you to make that choice?**

Keep a notebook for a year, journaling your observations about businesses and their strategies. What are their costs? What's their profit margin? What's their marketing strategy? Why do people choose their products or services? How do they keep customers coming back?

These questions will help you see how value is created and exchanged, giving you a wealth of ideas on generating income. Success starts with building a network of people who share your vision. Books alone cannot teach you all the nuances of business. You have to step out, make mistakes, and grow wiser through lived experiences.

How the Right People Shape Your Future

Success thrives in the right environment. Surround yourself with people who inspire, challenge, and support your vision. Attend events, workshops, or conferences where like-minded individuals gather. These places are perfect for exchanging ideas, learning from others, forming valuable connections, and creating something meaningful together. The people you meet can open doors, offer insights you'd never uncover alone, and collaborate in ways that drive progress.

Be proactive, introduce yourself, ask thoughtful questions, and listen. Relationships are built on trust, shared values, and mutual growth. Your environment shapes your potential, so cultivate it intentionally, surrounding yourself with people and opportunities that elevate your journey.

Paths to Generating Income:

Invest in Yourself:
The smartest investment is in your growth. Sharpen your skills and expand your knowledge to increase your future income. Every step you take today sets the stage for greater rewards tomorrow.

Turn Hobbies into Income:
What you love can become your income. From art to gaming or fitness, turn your passions into profitable ventures that pay you while you enjoy what you do.

Rent or Share Assets:
Use what you own to generate extra income. Rent out items like bikes, cars, or even tools to people who need them, turning unused assets into cash flow.

Build Your Personal Brand:
Establish yourself as a trusted figure in your field. Create content, offer advice, and share experiences that position you as an expert, leading to higher-paying opportunities and partnerships.

Offer Freelance Services:
If you have a skill, offer it to businesses and individuals. From graphic design to writing, web development, and marketing, freelancing is a flexible way to earn and build a portfolio.

Launch a Crowdfunding Campaign:
If you have an innovative product or idea, consider crowdfunding to raise the capital you need. Successful campaigns can generate not only income but also a community of supporters.

Affiliate Marketing:
Promote products or services you trust and earn commissions by recommending them, without the need to manage inventory.

Want more strategies? Created to help you and save time! Scan QR-CODE and download 100 Path$ to Generating Income content also explore additional resources at magicofgoal.com or follow me on social media: @mylifexsoul.

Every path starts somewhere. For example, trading time might be your first step, but over time, you can transition to selling knowledge or creating products. The key is to start taking small steps toward a vision that fits your life and goals.

If you're a young entrepreneur, don't fear failure. In fact, the person who becomes successful is often the one who has failed repeatedly. It's those who embrace failure, learn from it, and keep moving forward who build great businesses. The key is persistence. The best entrepreneurs are the ones who fail, reflect, and evolve over and over again.

Failure isn't the end. It's just a step on the way to success. Sometimes, the path to success even goes through failure, shame, mistakes, or setbacks. The most important thing is to gain valuable lessons along the way and keep moving forward.

When people look at the end product, they assume it's the result of an incredible person who was born that way, but they ignore the background and choices. **No one is jealous of how you got there. After all, when you look back on life, you either did or didn't take that step—action, said a word, wrote, or found a reason.**

What actions are you taking to create success? Simply thinking about it won't bring results. Yes, you may be involved in the process, but without clear actions, you're not moving forward. Many fail because they lack the resilience to withstand the challenges along the way.

To change your life, you don't have to win the lottery. You need to make a decision to stop being who you were, log into an operating system that contains subconscious applications, and then clearly formulate a model of a new self.

Turn No into Yes: Speak to Their Desires

When you're starting a business or trying to sell something you deeply believe in, it's easy to feel defeated when results don't show up. But here's the truth, no sales or lack of interest isn't rejection, it's redirection. It's a sign that you need to improve, not give up.

Sales and interest are not just about offering a product, they're about solving a problem in a way that resonates deeply with your target audience.

If sales aren't happening, ask yourself these key questions:

- What is my target audience?
- Do I truly understand my target audience's pain points, desires, and beliefs?
- Am I solving a real problem that people care about, or what can I bring into their lives that might make a meaningful difference or impact?

1. What emotions or motivations drive them to consider buying?
2. What's their journey and experience before, during, and after purchase?
3. Does my offer, branding, and product's value speak to them personally and touch them in a way that inspires them to take action?

- How will they feel after purchase, using my product?
- Does my offer align with the results, desires, triggers, and solutions they're looking for?

Sales are about connection, not just conversion. Your marketing should feel like a conversation, where you're addressing their needs in a way that speaks directly to them.

Next, pay attention to your thinking. Confidence in your offer is essential. Do you believe in your product's value? If not, work on rediscovering why you started and on the offer you're providing. Confidence is magnetic, and when you carry it, others will notice.

Ask yourself: What's your unique value proposition? How will you stand out? Sometimes, people prefer not just a product, but from whom they buy it—your personality can be your advantage.

"Do not be in the selling business, the worst thing you could ever do is just want to sell something to somebody. **You want to be in the reorder business.** So that the quality of your service or your product is so good **that the people who use it will want to reorder it or tell friends about it.**" – John Paul Dejoria (self-made billionaire).

Don’t chase the sale, serve the customer. Focus on how you can better serve your audience, even if it means changing your offering, adjusting your strategy, or improving the way you communicate a message. Consistent action, feedback, and a willingness to change when necessary create momentum.

The path to sales success starts with listening, adapting, and owning your value. Your lack of results doesn’t define your journey, it refines it. Now, focus on questions that reveal true needs and opportunities, keep creating value, and trust that the right customers will follow.

The best thing you can do to improve your mindset is to read successful people’s biographies, books, articles, movies, podcasts, etc. It will help you understand how they think and apply their experiences and methods to your life.

A book is like meeting a person because, if you think deeper, you can't meet them in person. It's your opportunity to learn, grow, and benefit from their experiences and methods.

"We don't start because it's hard, but it's hard because we don't start."

— Stoic philosophy

"Share this message, uplift others, and create change. Together, we grow. Mention @mylifexsoul in your story!"

I'd like to share insights from a conversation with a successful businessman. I won't disclose his name for privacy reasons, but I recognize that everyone's journey is unique, and their thoughts and advice may vary. I'm grateful to the Universe and God for pushing me out of my comfort zone and seizing opportunities that have broadened my perspective. Looking back, I don't regret the choices I made. They led me to this moment of growth and clarity.

1. "Know what drives you and keep money out of your primary focus, though you must manage it wisely."
2. "Consistency in a job you're passionate about yields results."
3. "Setting goals like becoming a billionaire or millionaire is not a goal. The sad thing is that people look for themselves in them and forget about themselves. It's vital to remember yourself when you are striving for wealth."
4. "Hard-earned money is more secure. It should be earned through diligent work, understanding that more money often brings more challenges."
5. "Ask yourself: Does your job allow you to live freely? Is it meaningful to you?"
6. "Investors seek potential. Meeting a billionaire who values your work can be a lottery."
7. "To rise, surround yourself with successful individuals and learn from them."
8. "Relationships thrive on respect and trust before love can truly blossom."
9. "Value time, as life passes swiftly like a single long day."

I am grateful for the opportunity to connect and for the time he invested in me. It's interesting to think that the *"future you"* may look back on this moment, on doubts and fears, and smile. Now, I can see how it all aligns with where I am today. So, make the choice now, embrace life, and act boldly.

YOU CAN DO IT, YOU CAN DO IT, YOU CAN DO IT, YOU CAN DO IT!
YOU CAN DO IT, YOU CAN DO IT, YOU CAN DO IT, YOU CAN DO IT!
YOU CAN DO IT, YOU CAN DO IT, YOU CAN DO IT, YOU CAN DO IT!

8

YOU CAN DO IT, YOU CAN DO IT, YOU CAN DO IT, YOU CAN DO IT!
YOU CAN DO IT, YOU CAN DO IT, YOU CAN DO IT, YOU CAN DO IT!
YOU CAN DO IT, YOU CAN DO IT, YOU CAN DO IT, YOU CAN DO IT!

CHAPTER 8:
BEYOND HUMAN LIMITS

Installing 72% 

cout << "Initializing Future.exe..." << endl;

It is very difficult to understand who I am by simply philosophizing and reasoning about it, or by searching within myself. While inner exploration is important, it can be an incomplete path. To fully understand who I am, I need to boldly move toward a specific goal, something concrete that aligns with my true purpose and passions.

Beyond the Body: Who Are We Really?

My opinion is that some people create an idea of themselves based on what they see. This means external confirmation where there is an influence not only on what you think about yourself and accept your beauty, but also on what people think about you.

There are also some people who tend to base their self-images on their inner world. But what unites them all? ***"CONVICTION."*** Is it true who we are, or is it all just a belief of ourselves? Let me tell you the story of a man, and his name is Thomas Edison.

One day, Thomas Edison came home from school and gave his mother a letter from his teacher. “Your son is a genius. This school is too small, and there are no teachers here who can teach him anything. Please teach him by yourself.”

Many years after his mother's death *(Edison was already one of the greatest inventors of the century)*, one day he was looking through the old family archives again and came across this letter. He opened it and read, “Your son is mentally retarded. We can no longer teach him in school with everyone else. Therefore, we recommend that he should be educated at home on his own.”

Edison cried for hours. Then he wrote in his diary, “Thomas Alva Edison was a mentally retarded child. Thanks to his heroic mother, he became one of the greatest geniuses of his age.”

What if I told you that in life it matters what decisions you make, but just as much it matters what people you meet in your life, and that's the sum of your life.

Do you see obstacles as failure?

"I have not failed. I've just found 10,000 ways that won't work."

– Thomas Edison

"Share this message, uplift others, and create change. Together, we grow. Mention @mylifexsoul in your story!"

The "View from the Future" Technique

It is believed that a person's thoughts before going to bed can have a strong effect on his unconscious. What if you learn how to manage this process?

There is an excellent NLP technique that got its start in the far 70s, when the creator of NLP, John Grinder, studied the behavioral and mental strategies of Nobel laureates. It turned out that there were several personality traits that united them. And one of them is, "They could dream the same way."

As a result, one technology was born, which over time, they were able to improve and turn into a working tool. **This technique is called "Looking from the future," and now everyone can use it to achieve the desired results.**

Before Bed Visualization: As you prepare to sleep, imagine yourself five or ten years into the future. Initially, observe this scenario dissociated, like watching a movie of your future self. Dissociation helps you perceive future achievements without overwhelming emotions. Now you're watching a movie from your own body. Look at your arms, legs, and everything around you.

Visualize it's a morning from the future and you open your eyes. Think about various aspects of your life: family, career, business, health, and finances. Picture yourself having achieved all your goals and feeling genuinely fulfilled and happy. Consider the people around you, the environment you live in, your financial status, and other significant details.

Embrace the Feeling: Engage emotionally with this future vision. Feel the joy, satisfaction, and fulfillment of having accomplished your dreams. Let this positive emotion sink in as you drift off to sleep. Is this exactly what you want?

If everything suits you, then proceed to the next step.

Combining focus and intention, mastering this technique allows you to harness the power of your subconscious mind to manifest your desired future and align your actions with your aspirations. Turn back to yourself today, who is now lying in bed or sitting on a chair.

Tell yourself:

- *How exactly did you get all this?*
- *What were you doing?*
- *How did you achieve this?*
- *What qualities and skills did you begin to own?*
- *Where will I end up if I keep moving with my current momentum? Am I truly happy with where it's taking me?*
- *Now look through the eyes of your future self. What would you say to the person you are today?*
- *What would be your next action?*

Ideally, you should write down all of your thoughts, tips, and steps to achieve your goal. If you are deeply immersed in your image of the future, then believe me. You will have something to say to yourself. You may even be surprised by such detailed feedback

When you tap into the power of your subconscious, you begin to see that the answers you need are already inside you. Trust yourself and the process. You are not a passive observer, but the creator of your future. Every step you take, no matter how small, shapes your destiny. Challenges will come, but they are opportunities to learn and grow. With each step forward, you're one step closer to turning your dreams into reality. Trust in your abilities, take action, and keep moving toward your goals. Your future is in your hands.

The Process of Achieving Goals

NEW WISH – A BIGGER GOAL

IMPROVING SELF-ESTEEM. INCREASING SELF-CONFIDENCE, FREQUENCY OF ENERGY!

NO ONE IS JEALOUS OF HOW YOU GOT THERE!

AWARD

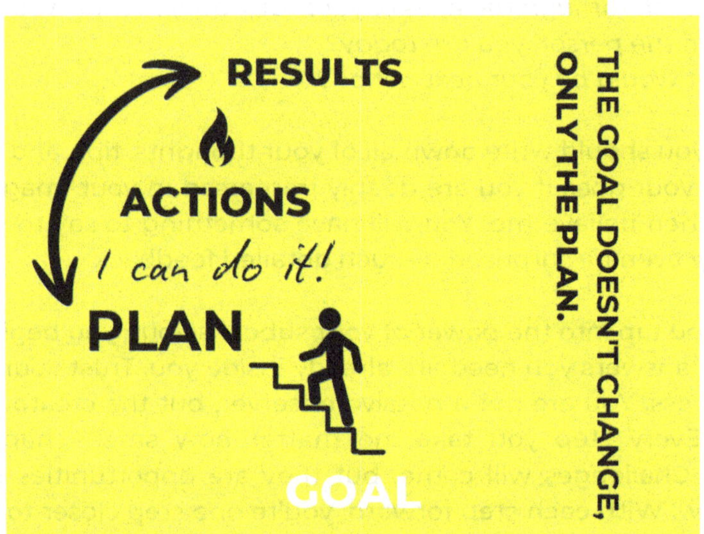

DESIRE / WANT *(TAKEN RESPONSIBLY!)*

The Goal must be energized with inner energy – preparedness!

GOAL – WHAT? TASK – HOW?

"Share this message, uplift others, and create change. Together, we grow. Mention @mylifexsoul in your story!"

"Victory is reserved for those who are willing to pay its price."
— Sun Tzu

SUCCESS

ACTION

PLAN

GOAL

VISION

Only your next step matters! We've all had bad days.

"If you are looking for the love of your life, stop. They will be waiting for you when you start doing things you love. Stop overanalyzing. Life is simple."
— The Holstee Manifesto

Space for Your Notes:

YOU CAN DO IT, YOU CAN DO IT, YOU CAN DO IT, YOU CAN DO IT!
YOU CAN DO IT, YOU CAN DO IT, YOU CAN DO IT, YOU CAN DO IT!
YOU CAN DO IT, YOU CAN DO IT, YOU CAN DO IT, YOU CAN DO IT!

YOU CAN DO IT, YOU CAN DO IT, YOU CAN DO IT, YOU CAN DO IT!
YOU CAN DO IT, YOU CAN DO IT, YOU CAN DO IT, YOU CAN DO IT!
YOU CAN DO IT, YOU CAN DO IT, YOU CAN DO IT, YOU CAN DO IT!

CHAPTER 9:
POINT A TO POINT B: YOUR GOAL JOURNEY

Installing 80%

"It's not the goal that transforms you. It's the person you become along the way."

— Unknown

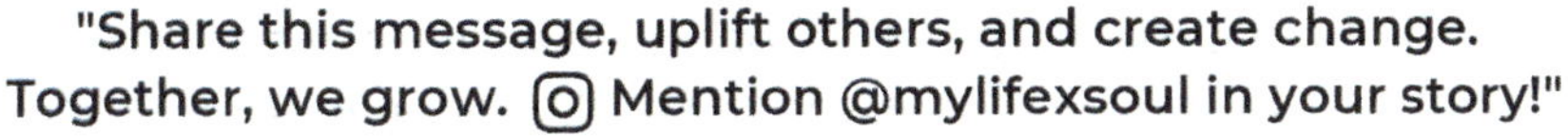

"Share this message, uplift others, and create change. Together, we grow. Mention @mylifexsoul in your story!"

"Time is worth our lives.
We analyze too much and
think, will it work or not?
Enough, stop wondering.
Start acting!"
— Unknown

Life is too short to wait..

"Share this message, uplift others, and create change.
Together, we grow. Mention @mylifexsoul in your story!"

Point A to Point B

What kind of magic has to happen for me to get from *"Point A"* to my desired *"Point B"*? Step.

The main reason why people fail to achieve their goals is the fear of failure. It is funny that the thought of failure comes when we do not have a clear idea of how to achieve it.

It's even ridiculous when we set a goal in an infinite time span, with no deadlines, and as a result postpone things for tomorrow. How valuable it is to retain this ability to walk the earth, rather than floating in the clouds all the time.

Have you ever noticed how difficult it is to stay motivated when you don't know what you're working toward? Lack of clarity often drains energy faster than physical exertion. On the other hand, when you have a clear goal, your mind sharpens, your decisions become easier, and your energy naturally aligns to move you forward.

To sustain energy, you need both the big picture and the small wins. The big picture gives you vision—your *"Point B."* The small wins along the way keep you motivated and build momentum. Whether it's crossing a task off your to-do list or hitting a significant milestone, progress fuels energy.

Think of energy as a flywheel. It takes effort to get it moving, but once it's spinning, it generates its own force. The same applies to your goals, the hardest part is starting. After that, momentum does the hard work.

Your mind is a powerful source of energy. When you visualize, you're not just imagining a better future, you're wiring your brain to believe it's achievable. When you embrace this belief, it creates a deep emotional connection to your goals, driving the energy and determination to take consistent action toward their achievement.

Every small action compounds, every moment of effort adds up, and before you know it, you'll be living the life you've always envisioned. Keep going! Your future is waiting for you to claim it.

I CAN DO IT, I CAN DO IT, I CAN DO IT, I CAN DO IT, I CAN DO IT!

Where Does Our Energy Come From?

Take some time to reflect on what truly matters to you in life. What are your core values, beliefs and priorities? Consider different areas of your life, such as your career, health, relationships, and personal development. What do you want to achieve in each of these areas?

So, my solution was to create clarity out of chaos. The word and the feeling of *"CLARITY"* is what leads us to our goal—final destination. However, we must also remember that clarity without action is like a basketball player without the ball. Clarity and action are partners, like the knight and the sword. Without action, clarity does not exist. Before we take the next step, let me share some information.

It has been revealed that people who can't reach a goal for years have had these mistakes. The biggest problem is not to set a point but to get there. People do not come to what they want because they lack the energy to try and make a stable action because the goal does not have any feelings. People don't reach what they want because of negative attitudes. We have been educated wrongly.

I wholeheartedly believe that you know what you want, but for some reason, we focus on the external picture instead of the internal. Just think about the feeling you want to experience, and you will create a goal or destination. Determine with feelings what we truly want to feel.

Did God create us to experience the world? To feel.

Your energy is your greatest asset, and its source lies in the alignment of your goals, purpose, and actions. When you find clarity, protect your focus, and build momentum, energy becomes a byproduct of your journey.

The answer isn't in chasing endless hacks or shortcuts. It's about connecting deeply with your purpose, visualizing your success, and taking consistent steps toward what truly matters. Energy doesn't come from external sources. It comes from within, fueled by the drive to get closer to your goals every day. So, rather than asking where energy comes from, ask yourself, how will I direct mine today?

Beyond the Fog: I Feel Lost

A sense of loss occurs when you feel disconnected from yourself. External pressures from the environment, people, and societal norms can create a strong belief that something is wrong with you, overshadowing your ability to shape your own life.

Failure, however, provides us with opportunities to learn more about ourselves, and as we grow, our unmet goals can evolve. If you cannot change the situation, you can change your perspective on it. It always begins with introspection.

Let's piece together the puzzle.

Consider this challenging example:

Profile: John

John is unsure of his ambitions, is surrounded by a negative environment and sets himself undefined goals. **Faced with the results, he becomes depressed and has suicidal thoughts, which he keeps to himself.** John often feels stuck in a stagnant life. He works in an office but perceives his career as stuck. Although he wants to make a change, he lacks a clear understanding of his goals and motivations.

A recent discovery is a note detailing John's aspirations:

1) Be more successful.
2) Become richer.
3) Travel around the world.
4) Change my life.

Let's delve into John's goals in more detail!

Badly Defined Goals

- **Unspecified goal: "Be more successful."**

John has not defined what being successful means to him and has no specific criteria for success.

- **Unspecified goal: "Become richer."**

John wants to improve his financial situation, but doesn't know how to do it.

- **Unspecified goal: "To travel the world."**

John dreams of world travel but does not consider his limited resources of time and money.

- **Unspecified goal: "Change my life."**

John feels that his life needs a change, but doesn't know what kind of change he wants to make or what he is working toward.

Solutions:

Unspecified goal: "Be more successful."

Solution: You know the saying, "Show me your friends, and I'll tell you your future." Success isn't just about hard work. It's also about the people you surround yourself with. If John wants to be more successful, he needs to build relationships with people who are positive, ambitious, and have the mindset he aspires to. Networking with the right individuals can open doors, offer fresh perspectives, and lead to new opportunities.

Defined Goal - Action Plan:

"I will make 10 meaningful connections with like-minded, ambitious people over the next three months. I will attend at least two networking events or join online communities each month where I can meet people who inspire me. Building a supportive network, I will surround myself with individuals who motivate me to take action and push me toward success."

Unspecified goal: "Become richer."
Solution: John should set a goal to save $200 per month for the next six months in a separate savings account. Additionally, he should invest in learning a new skill that could lead to higher-paying job opportunities or launch a side hustle, like offering freelance services or starting an online business.

Defined Goal - Action Plan:

"I will save $200 every month for the next 6 months and spend 5 hours each week learning a skill that can help me earn more. After 6 months, I'll use my new skill to either get a higher-paying job or start a side hustle."

Unspecified goal: "Travel around the world."
Solution: To make this dream a reality, John should first narrow down his destinations. Instead of thinking about traveling to the whole world at once, he should choose the top 5 countries he most wants to visit. For now, let's focus on just one country. Focusing on one destination makes the goal more manageable and actionable.

Defined Goal - Action Plan:

"I will choose one country, Japan, to visit within the next 12 months. I will create a budget and start saving $400 per month. Over the next 6 months, I will research and plan my trip, including flights, accommodation, and activities. In 12-months mark, I will have the necessary funds and all plans in place to visit Japan for at least two weeks."

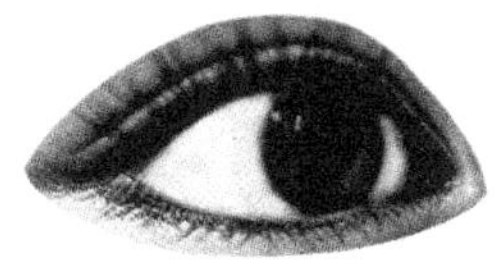

Unspecified goal: "Change my life."
Solution: To start changing his life, John should focus on tracking his progress daily. He can use a success journal to write down his daily wins, no matter how small. This will keep him motivated and allow him to reflect on how far he's come. Additionally, every Sunday, he should revise his journal to assess what went well and identify areas for improvement. This process will help him stay focused, grow, and make more informed decisions on how to keep moving forward.

Defined Goal - Action Plan:

"I will start a success journal and write down 3 tasks related to my goals that I need to accomplish each day. Every Sunday, I will review my journal and analyze what went well and where I can improve.

I will ask myself:

- *What achievements did I make?*
- *What difficulties did I face?*
- *What is my plan for the next week?*

After 30 days, I will review my progress and adjust my actions to ensure continuous growth and improvement."

You Know What You Truly Want!

Let's begin with something fundamental. The world is full of distractions, chaos, and endless noise, making it easy to lose sight of what really matters. But here's the trick! Instead of focusing on all the things pulling you in different directions, focus on one thing, the feelings and senses you want to experience.

These are the things that define your true desires, beyond surface-level wants and needs. Take a mindful moment to reflect. What 3 feelings or senses matter most to you? Maybe it's inner peace, or the deep fulfillment that comes from self-realization. Whatever it is, let it guide your choices every day. The clearer your purpose, the more effortlessly your decisions will align. If you want self-realization, do whatever aligns with it and feels right for you.

Now, take a moment to sit down, close your eyes, and dream. Write it all down. What you put on that paper is the roadmap to your dream future. Ask yourself, what kind of life do you want in 5 to 10 years? Then, bring your vision closer by asking what you want in the next 1 to 3 years. Narrow it down even further to 3 to 5 months and finally focus on the next month. This exercise isn't just about goals, it's about understanding the bigger picture and connecting it to today. And here's the surprise, the goal of today, the one that will shape your tomorrow.

Yes, what you plant today will grow into your tomorrow. As you gain clarity, your life becomes more meaningful, motivated, and driven. You'll begin to understand your actions and nurture a deeper desire to move forward.

Many people wait for the ***"perfect moment"*** to start. They think they need more time, more knowledge, or more resources. But the perfect moment never arrives because the best time to start is now. Right where you are. The seeds for all great achievements are planted in the present, not in some ideal future scenario.

"Point A" doesn't have to be a place of perfection. It's just the beginning. It's where you acknowledge your current reality, accept where you are, and commit to the journey ahead. The most powerful shift happens when you stop waiting for the "right moment" and simply choose to take the first step.

We often set goals like, “I want to be successful,” “I want to be happy,” or “I want to make a lot of money.” But these wishes, while typical, are often too broad to guide us effectively. **Your *"Point B"* needs to be specific, measurable, and motivating.**

Defining your destination clearly isn’t just about creating a roadmap. It’s about having a vision that excites you enough to pull you through the tough moments.

Ask yourself, what does success look like to me? Why do people imagine success as a straight line from Point A to Point B? But in reality, it’s rarely that simple. The journey is filled with setbacks, highs and lows, and where you feel completely lost and unheard. Don’t be discouraged by the messiness of the journey. Embrace it.

Every failure, every stumble, and every challenge on your path is simply a hidden lesson. When you meet obstacles, instead of asking, “Why is this happening to me?” ask, **“What can I learn from this? How can I grow from this experience?”** Each obstacle strengthens you and brings you closer to your destination.

A Moment Between Us

Do you think the path to writing a book was clear? For me, it wasn’t. **I spent days and nights writing, creating, and combining ideas, but I enjoyed every moment because, as I’ve said, it was part of a greater mission, something I truly believed in.**

It was all about taking action, step by step, and learning from failures along the way. It’s a journey many of us go through. But now, here you are, reading this book. In this moment, are you grateful for the words on these pages? If you are, it means so much to hear that.

You know what? From the very first moment I started writing, I felt confident, even though the path ahead was unclear. I was willing to give my time, time that can never be returned. It felt strange, yet beautiful, something new yet deeply right, as if it was exactly what I was meant to do. This is the secret, trusting your intuition, your soul, before you fully understand it and allowing it to guide you to something far greater than you ever imagined.

The Bamboo Lesson

The Wise Man leads You into a serene garden. Bamboo stalks sway gently in the wind, their tall, green frames reaching for the sky.

You: "Wise Man, this place feels... different. There's something alive about it that I can't quite explain. Why have you brought me here?"
Wise Man *(smiling)*:
"Every new soul must first understand the nature of this world before they can move through it. Today, your lesson is with the bamboo."

You *(tilting head)*:
"Bamboo? How can it teach me about this world?"
Wise Man *(gesturing to the tall stalks)*:
"Do you see these giants? For years, they grew only underground. Nothing appeared above the surface, though their roots spread deep and wide. Then, when they were ready, they shot up, reaching their height in a few weeks."

You *(surprised)*:
"That's incredible... but why wait so long?"
Wise Man *(smiling)*:
"Because strength comes from the unseen work. Without deep roots, they could never grow so tall. Remember this, growth begins where no one can see it."

You looks up at the bamboo, pondering its meaning.

Faith is the bridge between where you are and where you want to be. It's the belief that, even when you can't see the progress, it's happening. It's trusting the process when the outcome feels distant.

Think of an athlete training in the off-season. There's no crowd, no medal, no applause, just sweat and struggle. But when the new season begins, those invisible hours of hard work become the foundation of their success.

The same applies to relationships, careers, or personal growth. Faith keeps you watering the seed when logic tells you to stop. The bamboo's explosive growth isn't magic. It's the result of years of quiet work. And the same is true for you. Every hour you spend learning, practicing, failing, and trying again is an investment in your roots. One day, you'll look back on the journey and realize that the growth you thought was sudden was years in the making.

So the next time you feel stuck, when progress seems invisible, remember the bamboo. Its strength lies not only in how tall it grows but in the faith required to nurture its roots.

Your time is coming. Trust it.

"Share this message, uplift others, and create change. Together, we grow. Mention @mylifexsoul in your story!"

Overcoming the Big Elephant

In the context of achieving your big goals, this is the mindset you need. The *"big elephant"* represents your ultimate, seemingly huge goal, whether it's writing a book, starting a business, or achieving a lifelong dream. When you look at the elephant as a whole, it can feel scary, even impossible. But the truth is, true success isn't achieved all at once.

It's about breaking that elephant down into smaller steps and taking them one by one. Every step you take brings you closer. It's about persistence, focus, and not getting overwhelmed by the size of the task. Just like eating an elephant, achieving your big goal isn't about doing everything at once. It's about taking steady, consistent action.

So, what's your elephant? What's that big, bold goal you've set for yourself? Don't focus on how big it seems. Instead, commit to the first step and keep going, one bite at a time.

Remember, progress isn't always a straight line. There will be setbacks, detours, and moments of doubt. But as long as you keep taking action, even when it feels like you're not making much progress, you'll look back and realize how far you've come.

The key is not to rush, not to force things to happen, but to trust the process and enjoy the journey, no matter how long it takes. Keep breaking that elephant down into manageable pieces, and soon enough, you'll have eaten the whole thing. Success will no longer seem so far away.

- [x] I can!
- [ ] I will!
- [ ] Watch me!

Facing the Big Elephant: A Step-by-Step Morning Run

Let's say your big goal is to go running every morning. The night before, you plan to wake up early and start your run, but when the morning comes, you're hit with a wave of laziness. You didn't take the time to remind yourself why you want to run, and now your motivation is low.

But here's the gift. Inside your mind, you hear a dialogue, a conversation that gently guides you forward, step by step:

- I want to run, but I'm feeling lazy.
- Okay, can I get out of bed?
- I can, and I have the opportunity.
- Can I get dressed?
- I can.
- Can I put on my shoes?
- I can.
- Can I walk outside?
- I can.
- Can I walk 10 steps?
- I can.
- Can I increase the speed?
- I can.
- How about some music?
- Maybe that will help. Oh, yes!
- Before you realize it, you're already on your way!
- Wait, what?
- Oh, yes, you can!

Even when immediate resources or clear paths are unavailable, developing a strong character can propel you toward your goal. As you cultivate these qualities, you prepare yourself to seize opportunities when they arise, and to turn your aspirations into reality when the right time comes.

Character lays the foundation for success, because it's not just about the circumstances, but about the person you become in the process.

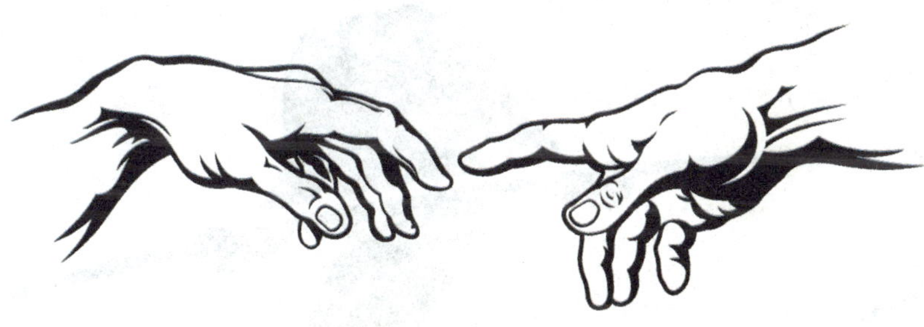

PUSH AND SUCCEED!

P - ***PRAY.***
U - ***UNTIL.***
S - ***SOMETHING.***
H - ***HAPPENS.***

+ TAKE ACTION!

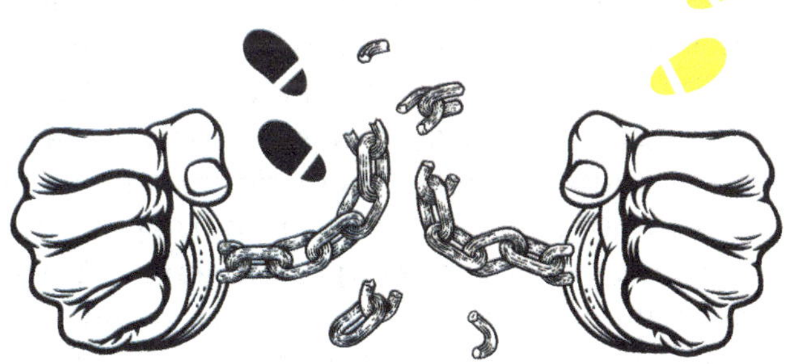

"Share this message, uplift others, and create change. Together, we grow. Mention @mylifexsoul in your story!"

It is the movement of a man walking on a tightrope. He is moving and swaying all the time, but he is moving forward. He does not take huge steps because then he would fall, unless he is an acrobat, and at the same time he does not stand still. Because the more we stand still, the more unstable we are.

Just like the man on the tightrope, life demands balance. You may sway, you may stumble, but as long as you keep moving forward, you're progressing. Don't be afraid of small steps. Every move you make, no matter how tiny, is a step closer to your dreams.

Remember, standing still only breeds doubt and instability. Keep your eyes on your goal, trust in your journey, and move with purpose. Success isn't about making giant leaps. It's about staying committed, even when the path seems uncertain. You have the strength within you to keep moving, one step at a time.

"Share this message, uplift others, and create change. Together, we grow. Mention @mylifexsoul in your story!"

YOU'RE THE CREATOR OF YOUR OWN PATH!
STOP
ONE WAY

YOU CAN DO IT, YOU CAN DO IT, YOU CAN DO IT, YOU CAN DO IT!
YOU CAN DO IT, YOU CAN DO IT, YOU CAN DO IT, YOU CAN DO IT!
YOU CAN DO IT, YOU CAN DO IT, YOU CAN DO IT, YOU CAN DO IT!

10

YOU CAN DO IT, YOU CAN DO IT, YOU CAN DO IT, YOU CAN DO IT!
YOU CAN DO IT, YOU CAN DO IT, YOU CAN DO IT, YOU CAN DO IT!
YOU CAN DO IT, YOU CAN DO IT, YOU CAN DO IT, YOU CAN DO IT!

LOW BATTERY – RECHARGE NOW!

CHAPTER 10: YOUR UNREALIZED PLANS

Installing 84%

Unleash!

THE POWER OF YOUR SPIRIT!

"Share this message, uplift others, and create change. Together, we grow. Mention @mylifexsoul in your story!"

4. Mission:

Try this simple experiment. All you need is a pen and paper. In the morning, write down your activities every hour throughout the day. Set a timer to remind you each hour and note what you did:

- Woke up.
- Prepared breakfast.
- Continue detailing each hour's activities until bedtime.
- In the evening, look at your notes and ask yourself: What could I have done differently? Am I happy with how the day went? We often go through our days without thinking. Tracking and reviewing your day helps you grow.

Each Sunday, summarize the week: What was accomplished? What wasn't? What's next? Treat yourself as your own company, just as big corporations do with their daily and weekly reviews.

Life isn't a game you've always played. Trying new methods can give you different results, as mentioned before.

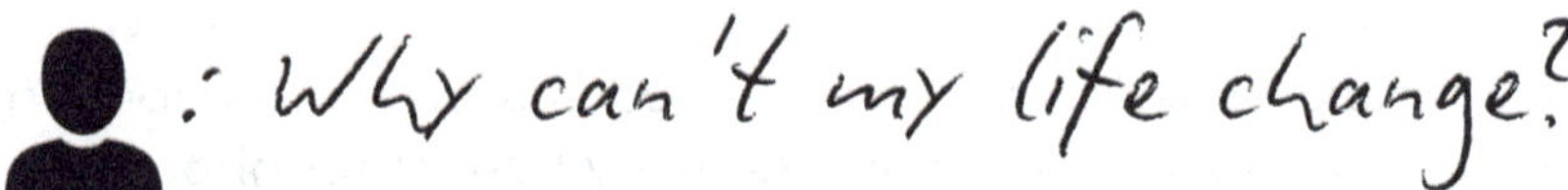

what about us?

GOALS ? IDEAS

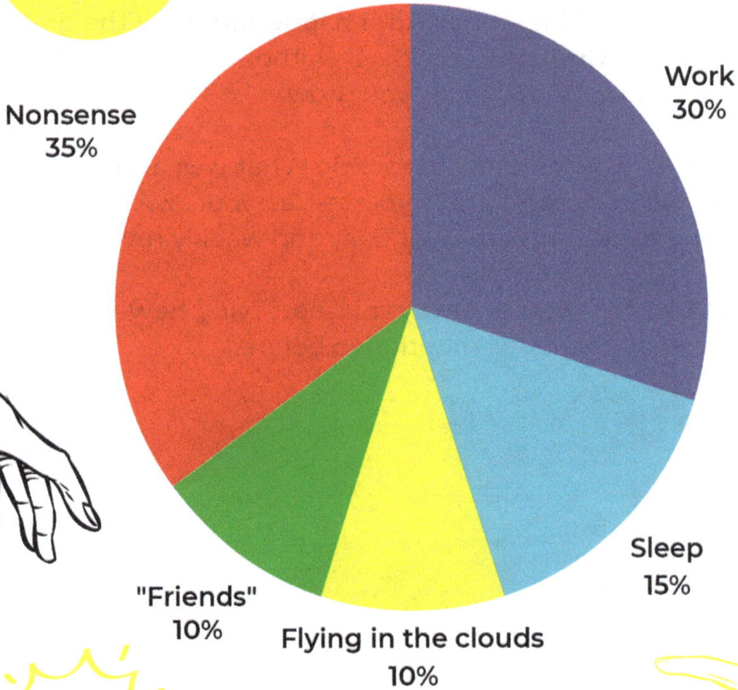

Nonsense 35%

Work 30%

Sleep 15%

Flying in the clouds 10%

"Friends" 10%

YEAH!

UNIVERSE : WHY YOU CAN'T CHANGE?

Life is a complicated thing.
: I'm just not that kind of person.
I can't achieve anything.

The Power of Focus in Life

Why do some people succeed and others don't understand what's wrong with me? The answer to this life-shaping question is the word ***"PRIORITIES."*** It makes sense if you don't take the time to achieve a goal, you won't achieve it.

As it was said in my philosophical example, you are already a billionaire. How many seconds are you willing to pay for? But do you want to pay? Where you direct your attention and your energy, it will grow.

It's like watering a flower. We take care of the surroundings of the flower, but we give the main focus of attention to the flower. Sad, but those who fail prefer to think but not to act. They dream and plan beautifully, but they always lack the push to act.

Stop dreaming and start acting. After all, in the beginning, you can carefully think everything through, but because of fear and your deep-rooted perfectionism, it may not work out, and the plan will have to be changed in accordance with current realities.

A successful person is flexible and on the move. I understand you and why you feel this way. I face similar thoughts myself, but let me tell you something.

This world is going to change a lot, but the one who realizes their mistakes and adapts their plans or direction the fastest will be the winner in the age of information technology and competition.

The tasks are as difficult as we imagine, as far as my weakness allows. The person does not understand this and quickly gives up. We make plans every year. Every year, we promise ourselves that I will work hard this year, and then we do it again. These plans are not destined to come true because we do not pay enough time to those tasks.

It's important to see things through to the end, and so it is in everything. It is better to do it and regret it than not to do it and regret it all your life. It's hard because you don't make a decision.

Treat everything you do with the care and attention you would give to something you deeply love, as if it were your own child.

Focus on Outcomes vs. Focus on the Process

We are often encouraged to dream big and focus on the results we want. Whether it's a successful career, a thriving business, or a healthier lifestyle, our goals are meant to inspire us. But here's a truth we don't always hear. Focusing solely on the outcome can leave you feeling empty and unfulfilled, even after achieving it.

Outcomes are like the destination on a map. They show us where we want to go and keep us moving forward. But the true essence of life lies in the journey itself. The process, the daily efforts, the setbacks, the small wins, and the growth that happens in between is where transformation unfolds.

When we obsess over results, we risk impatience and frustration. Every delay feels like failure, and every setback feels unbearable. Your self-worth becomes tied to whether or not you succeed. But the truth is, outcomes are fleeting. They are moments of success, but they don't last. The process, however, is what shapes us. It's where we build resilience, develop new skills, and learn to appreciate the journey.

Take the example of climbing a mountain. If all you care about is reaching the peak, every step feels like a chore. But if you embrace the climb, the sounds, the views, the progress, and the lessons learned from each challenge, you'll realize the journey itself holds as much value as the summit.

The peak is important, but the climb is what makes it meaningful. The process shapes you into the person who deserves the success waiting at the top.

This is where balance comes in. Set clear goals to guide you, but don't let them define you. Commit to the process. Trust that every small effort, every struggle, and every victory adds up to something bigger than the result itself. When you focus on the process, the outcome often takes care of itself. Success isn't a single moment in time. It's the byproduct of who you become through the journey.

What would your life look like if you stopped chasing results and started embracing the process? The steps you take each day shape you far more than the destination ever will.

The Art of Sharpening Your Focus

Focus is more than just an act of concentration. In today's world, there are so many things that claim our attention. We try to balance work, relationships, personal goals, and everything in between. With so much pulling us in different directions, it's easy to feel scattered. True success is built on the ability to focus deeply on what matters most.

Imagine a sharp knife. When it's well-honed, it can cut through even the toughest materials with ease. But a dull knife? It struggles and leaves a mess.

Your focus works in the same way. When you sharpen it, you can handle any task with precision and clarity. When it's unfocused, it's harder to make progress, and everything feels more difficult than it needs to be. The first step in sharpening your focus is to eliminate distractions. This means saying "no" to things that don't align with your goals, no matter how appealing they might seem. Distractions may appear small, but they compound over time, pulling you away from what truly matters. They can drain your energy and hold you back from reaching your full potential, making it harder to turn your dreams into reality.

Next, focus on one task at a time. Multitasking splits your attention and slows progress. When you give your full attention to something, you build momentum and move forward faster. Each focused effort compounds, bringing you closer to your goals.

Remember, focus is a muscle. The more you practice it, the stronger it becomes. At first, it might feel uncomfortable to block out distractions or narrow your attention to just one task.

But over time, it becomes easier, and your ability to concentrate will significantly skyrocket, enhancing your productivity. Sharpening your focus isn't just about working harder, but working smarter. It's about aligning your energy with your goals, taking intentional actions, and pushing through discomfort.

When you focus on the process, embrace new experiences, and keep moving forward with unwavering determination, you unlock your true potential and build the foundation for long-term success.

Stay Plugged In

One day, while sitting in a café, I wrote down a simple question: What does it mean to be a successful person? As I thought about it, my ideas started to flow, and I wrote them down.

I realized that we are much like phones that wake up fully charged each day, ready to unplug from the charger and operate on the energy we've stored.

Think of this. We begin our day with a full charge:
24 hours minus the 8 hours we spend sleeping, leaving us with 16 hours of energy to use. A successful person is someone who knows how to manage their energy, direct it wisely, maintain focus, and stay productive throughout the day.

Now, imagine a phone with multiple apps running in the background. It doesn't take long before the battery drains, and the phone is left with just a few hours of charge.

Life is similar. We face countless experiences: mistakes, victories, emotions, thoughts, actions, and distractions. In the midst of all of this, the question that truly matters is:
"What will be my next move?" You have a choice, do nothing and feel empty, or take action and feel tired but accomplished. Success lies in making the right choice. Success isn't measured by a big bank account. It's about staying connected to what truly matters. When you focus on what really counts, everything else falls into place.

Once a week, set aside an hour for a quiet moment. No phone, no music, no noise. In that silence, you may realize what you've been missing and gain clarity on where you want to go. These moments lead to profound personal growth.

The hard truth is that if you let distractions rule your life, you will never unleash your true potential, because you're wasting your most important power—your attention.

*Okay, my plans are falling apart.
This isn't what I wanted.
What can I do now to keep moving
in the direction I want?*

CHAPTER 11:
LOOKING FOR MOTIVATION?

Installing 88%

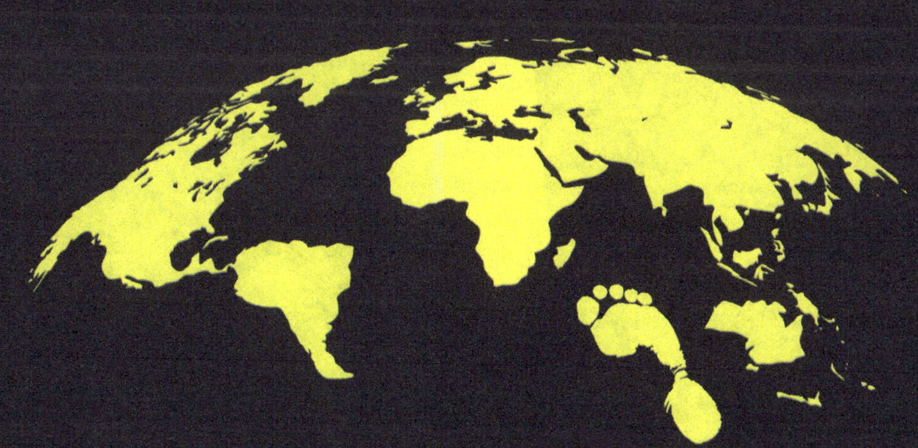

How **BIG** would you **DREAM** if you knew you couldn't fail?

"Share this message, uplift others, and create change. Together, we grow. Mention @mylifexsoul in your story!"

MOTIVATION

OLD
WAYS
WON'T OPEN
NEW
DOORS

MOTIVATION OR DISCIPLINE?

Most people seek motivation, but true success requires a clear *"Why?"* and a strong sense of discipline to overcome challenges and achieve goals. Motivation might spark the journey, but ultimate success depends on discipline, your decision, and unwavering commitment.

Discipline represents willpower in action, while motivation sparks your desire, discipline keeps you moving forward.

Remember, visualizing a goal energizes us because it gives our efforts meaning. Without meaning, there is no energy.

Motivation works best when you inspire others, but self-discipline is more effective for personal progress. During difficult times, when motivation is needed most, it can be summarized as going from pain to pleasure. It's crucial to negotiate with yourself rather than terrorize yourself. New solutions emerge in a state of calm, which is why maintaining calmness is so important.

The real question is not whether you are successful, but how many attempts it takes to reach your goal. Discipline is about self-control, prioritizing long-term rewards over short-term temptations that can distract you from your goals. It means training yourself to make smart choices now, knowing they will pay off in the future.

Consistency is the foundation of discipline, even if it's just small steps like dedicating 30 minutes a day to your goal. If you make a mistake, don't let it hold you back. Just keep moving forward. Your subconscious mind is like Aladdin's lamp, and you are the genie with the power to bring your dreams to life. **With time, effort, and focus, anything is possible.**

But how do you maintain the momentum toward your dreams?

"Share this message, uplift others, and create change. Together, we grow. Mention @mylifexsoul in your story!"

A temporary defeat simply reveals flaws in your plan, not your ability to succeed. Mastering yourself is the foundation of discipline. You can't control a situation until you first conquer your inner self. Without this, you're vulnerable to negative thoughts, emotions, and habits that can hold you back. To achieve success, you must learn to control these internal forces. This is the key to moving from failure to action.

At the level of action, when you hear an idea, you immediately take steps to make it happen. Your confidence allows you to act because you've trained yourself to move forward without hesitation. The main resource you have is your ability to bring yourself to that level of action.

When you make a decision, your mind works to find a solution. But when you remain uncertain or give in to negative emotions like worry or sadness, you let these states steer your life.

Success is determined by one thing: the choices you make.

Destiny may know the path, but every step is yours. Each decision shapes your journey, and the courage to take action defines your fate. In the end, it is not destiny that creates success, but your will to move forward.

It is about the vision you set, the steps you take, and the dedication and unwavering determination that turn dreams into reality.

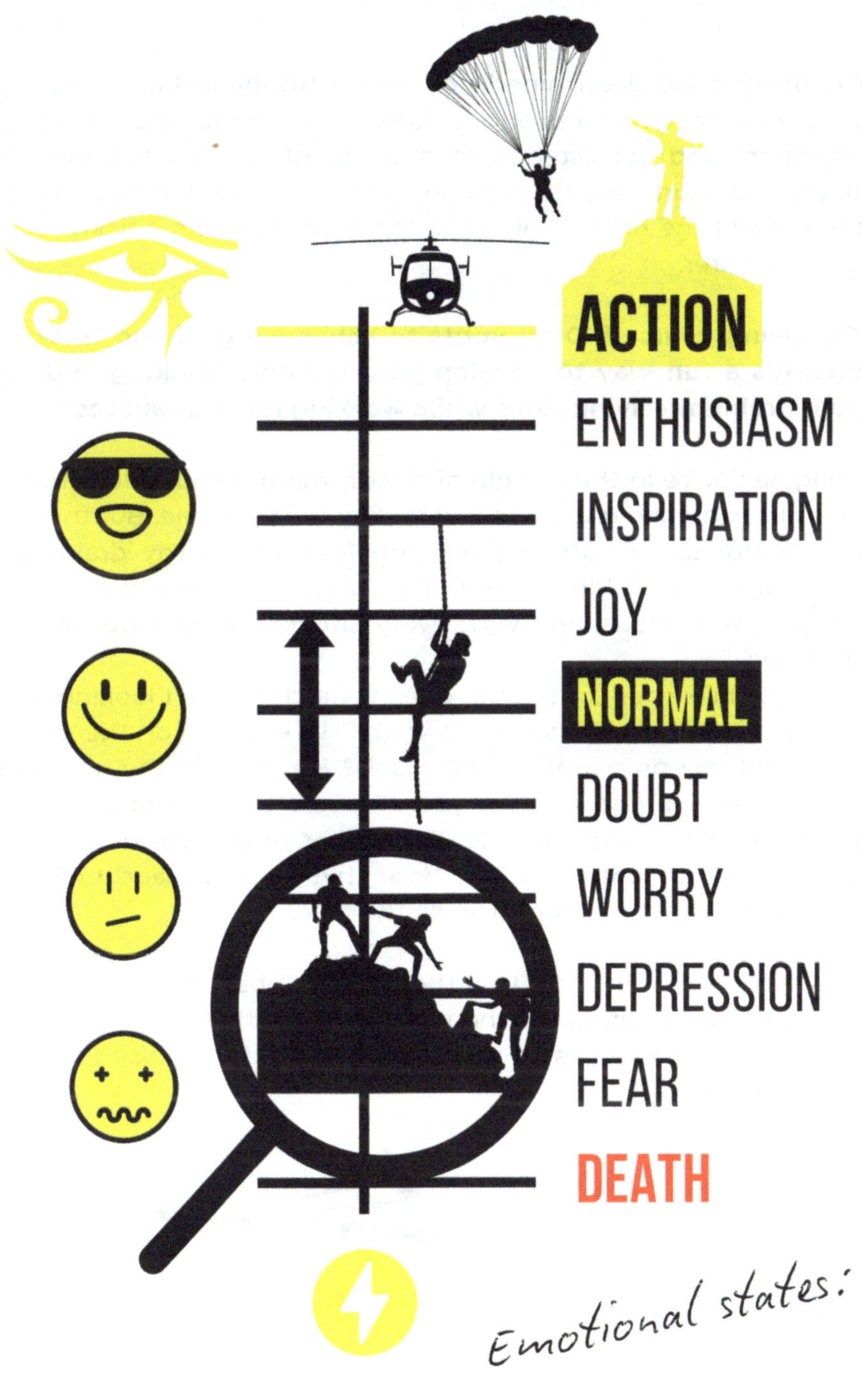
ACTION
ENTHUSIASM
INSPIRATION
JOY
NORMAL
DOUBT
WORRY
DEPRESSION
FEAR
DEATH
Emotional states:

Champions are determined not with a trophy in hand, but in the daily routine when no one is looking at them. Your focus, your attention, and consistency. In a world of too much information, news, and short clips, it's not enough that we find it difficult to focus for a long time on a single task. We expect results quickly, but we give up faster.

Try giving yourself 10 attempts to achieve a goal and track each one. It's a fun way to develop your creative thinking and boost your problem-solving skills while working towards success.

Imagine you're in the middle of a swimming competition. You're in first place, breaking records and feeling unstoppable. But then, your competitor starts catching up. You feel the energy drain as the thought hits you: "I'm losing!" That simple thought begins to eat away at your focus, and with every stroke, you feel weaker, more defeated.

Meanwhile, your competitor doesn't flinch. He isn't looking at your speed or comparing his race to yours. His eyes are on the prize, his focus entirely on winning. The result? He stays in rhythm, gliding forward with purpose while you struggle to keep up. This is the power of focus. When you let distractions or the fear of losing take over, your momentum is lost. Your rhythm is off, and before you know it, you're struggling to finish the race.

This serves as a reminder that the greatest obstacle in any race isn't the other competitors. It's the internal battle that can throw you off course. Keep your eyes on your own lane, and the finish line will be yours to cross.

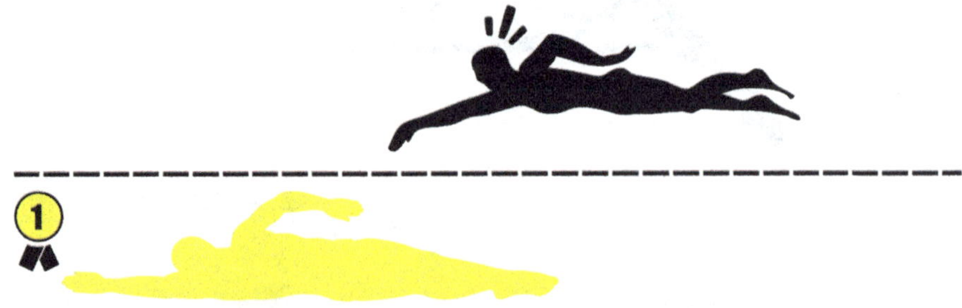

I CAN DO IT, I CAN DO IT, I CAN DO IT, I CAN DO IT, I CAN DO IT!

The Power of Planning

- **Prioritize Your Top 3 Tasks:** The evening before, identify the three most important things you want to accomplish tomorrow. This ensures that you're focused on what matters most and don't get sidetracked by less important tasks. Align these tasks with your long-term goals, so each step brings you closer to your bigger vision.

- **Gain Peace of Mind:** When you have a clear plan for tomorrow, your mind can let go of the worries and uncertainties that often keep you awake. This mental clarity allows you to relax, sleep deeply, and wake up confident, knowing exactly what lies ahead.

- **Start Your Day with Focus:** Imagine waking up with purpose, knowing exactly what needs to be done. A clear plan eliminates the stress of decision-making and immediately gives you a sense of direction. You'll start your day with momentum, ready to take on whatever comes your way.

Planning isn't just about setting goals. It's about creating a clear path to those goals, eliminating distractions, and taking action. When you set aside time to plan, you're investing in your own success and productivity.

Whenever you plan ahead, you're not just organizing your day. Instead, you're shaping your future. A simple plan helps clear your mind, reduces anxiety, and ensures you're always moving toward your bigger goals.

It's not about perfection, but about making consistent progress. With each small task completed, you build momentum. The act of planning helps you stay focused and makes the journey toward your success much more achievable.

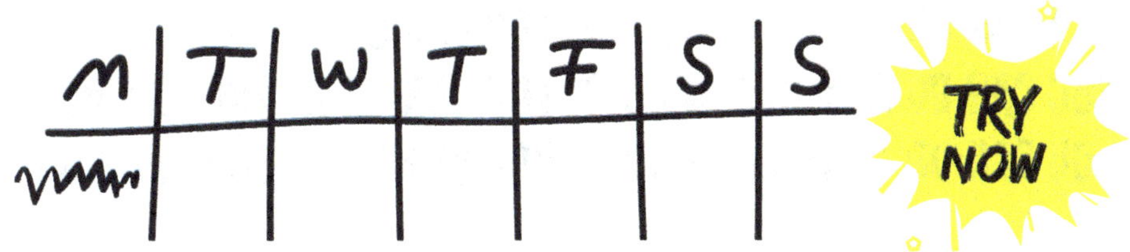

YOU CAN DO IT, YOU CAN DO IT, YOU CAN DO IT, YOU CAN DO IT!
YOU CAN DO IT, YOU CAN DO IT, YOU CAN DO IT, YOU CAN DO IT!
YOU CAN DO IT, YOU CAN DO IT, YOU CAN DO IT, YOU CAN DO IT!

12

YOU CAN DO IT, YOU CAN DO IT, YOU CAN DO IT, YOU CAN DO IT!
YOU CAN DO IT, YOU CAN DO IT, YOU CAN DO IT, YOU CAN DO IT!
YOU CAN DO IT, YOU CAN DO IT, YOU CAN DO IT, YOU CAN DO IT!

"Think of self-improvement as building your own real estate. Investing in growth boosts your value, while neglect, like an abandoned house, holds you back and stops you from reaching your full potential." — Evening Philosophy

"Share this message, uplift others, and create change. Together, we grow. Mention @mylifexsoul in your story!"

Thank You, Wise Man

You: "Thank you, Wise Man, for sharing so much with me. But where did you get such knowledge and wisdom?"
Wise Man *(smiling gently)*:
"The master has failed more times than the beginner has tried. You see, wisdom is born from failure, not success. Remember, I'll always be where the invisible is. Believe in the unseen, the invisible, the unknowable. But you'll always be closer if you act."

(It was a significant pause.)

Wise Man: "And thank you, for protecting me that day and for understanding the value of presence."
You: *(Silent, reflecting.)*
Wise Man: "I know you're quiet now, but one day, you'll wake up."
You: "Wake up? What do you mean?"
Wise Man *(smiling)*:
"It's getting late. I'm glad I could share this with you. Rest now. Tomorrow, your journey begins. The Dragon of Wishes is awaits."
You *(thinking to themselves)*:
"Why did he say "wake up"? What did he mean?"

CHAPTER 12:
DEATH: THE FINAL AWAKENING

The Final Lesson

You: "What a beautiful sunrise, Wise Man. Just look at this!"

But the Wise Man lay still, his eyes closed, holding a note in his hand.

You *(in shock)*:
"What is this?" (notices the Wise Man's stillness) "He's... he's dead!"

(You unfolds the note.)
Note:
"I felt that death would return, and perhaps it already has. I won't know unless I wake up. Remember this always, I'll be where the invisible is. Believe in the unseen, the invisible, the unknowable. But you'll always be closer if you act.

I have a favor to ask. Leave me here and close the door. Take the emerald ring from my finger. It's yours now.

Thank you for everything. You are the chosen one."

You *(say, confused)*:
"The chosen one? But... I still have so many questions."

The morning light streams through the window, casting a glow on the note in your hand. The words echo in your mind:
"Believe in the unseen... But you'll always be closer if you act."

You clench the note in your hand, take a deep breath, with one last look at the Wise Man, you whisper, "Thank you."

As the door closes behind you, you realize it's not the end, but the first step toward... a new chapter, waiting to unfold.

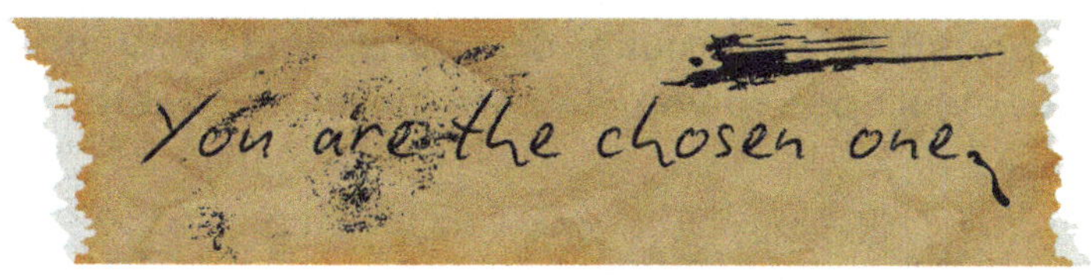

In the Shadow of Death

Many see death as an end, cruel and inevitable, yet throughout life, we experience countless small deaths. Parts of who we were fade away to make room for who we are becoming. Each moment presents a choice to remain as we are and stay comfortable, or to step into the unknown and embrace change.

Cemeteries hold a unique richness, not because of what is buried there, but because of the countless untold stories, unspoken words, unfulfilled dreams, unwritten books, and unrealized potential left behind. These are the priceless treasures the world never got to see.

So, what gives life its true value? In a world defined by connections and contributions, will you be remembered for the impact you made or forgotten as the world moves on? Life cannot simply be about existing and then fading away. There is a purpose within you, a spark that shapes the world around you, lighting the way and revealing your unique gifts.

The greatest tragedy is not failure. Failure teaches, grows, and transforms. A life without goals, passion, or a sense of purpose is its own kind of death. Yet even this death can hold the seed of freedom. Letting go of fear and doubt can lead to the kind of life that feels truly alive.

We all face the same inevitable end, but our legacies are shaped by what we choose to leave behind. Your story is written in the dreams you chase, the ideas you share, and the talents you nurture. These become the echoes of your existence, carrying on long after you are gone. A life's end is defined by the truths we hold, which vary from person to person.

I invite you to live with intention, take risks, and leave behind a story worth remembering. Life's final chapter will come. So, what are you waiting for? Every moment is an opportunity to write your own chapter. Don't wait for the perfect moment—create it.

Use your potential and make decisions, and new doors and opportunities will open to you. You are more than death!

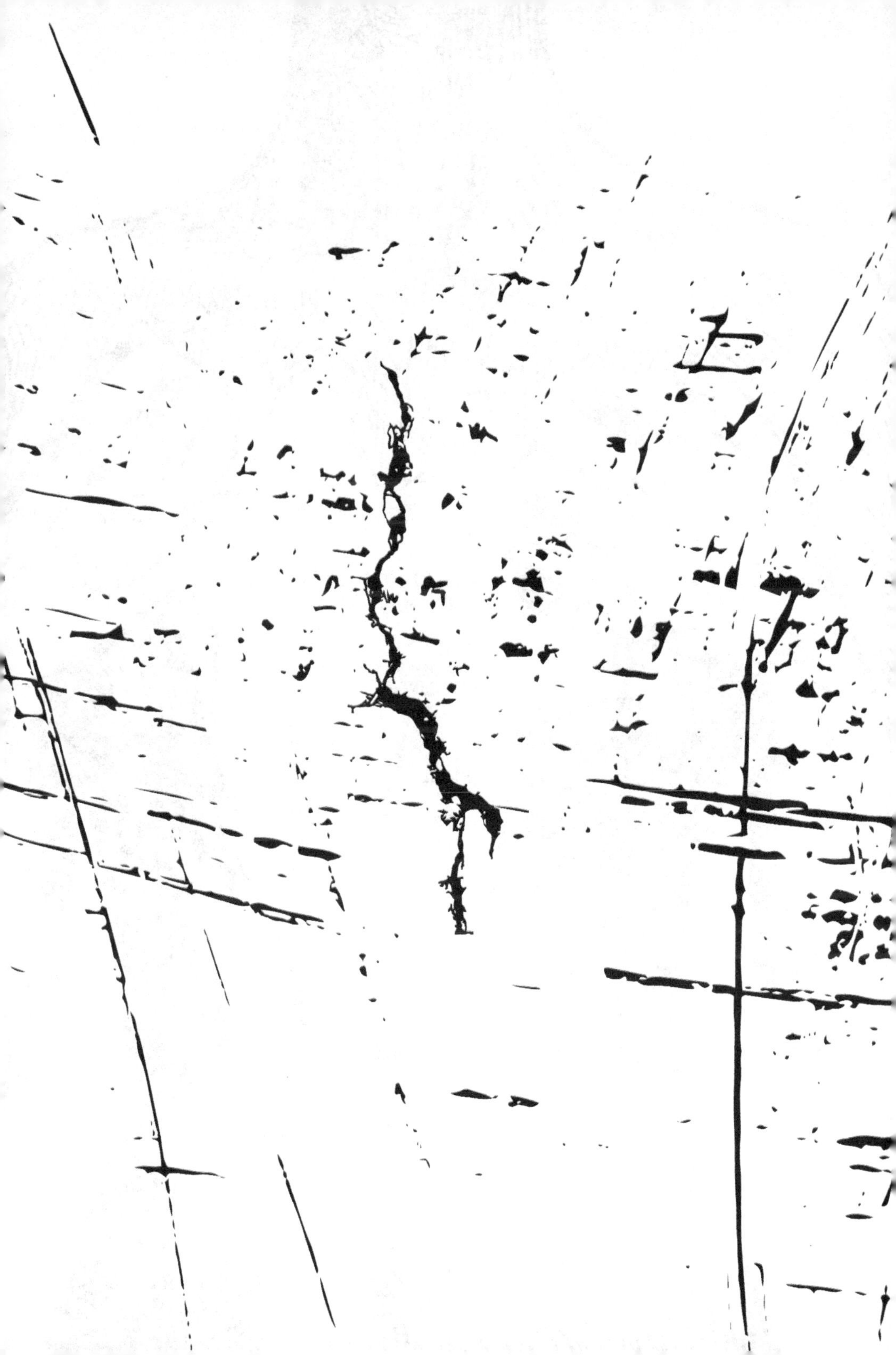

Look into the mirror.
This is where change begins:
the awakening of your true power.

When you embrace your true self, you'll discover the warrior within. You are stronger, more strategic, and more resilient than you've ever realized. Every challenge you face is an opportunity to tap into that inner strength, to grow even more powerful, and to rise above any limitations. The strength you seek is already inside you, waiting to be unleashed. Remember, the challenges ahead aren't obstacles, they are your greatest opportunities to demonstrate your true power and limitless potential.

"Share this message, uplift others, and create change. Together, we grow. Mention @mylifexsoul in your story!"

YOU CAN DO IT, YOU CAN DO IT, YOU CAN DO IT, YOU CAN DO IT!
YOU CAN DO IT, YOU CAN DO IT, YOU CAN DO IT, YOU CAN DO IT!
YOU CAN DO IT, YOU CAN DO IT, YOU CAN DO IT, YOU CAN DO IT!

13

YOU CAN DO IT, YOU CAN DO IT, YOU CAN DO IT, YOU CAN DO IT!
YOU CAN DO IT, YOU CAN DO IT, YOU CAN DO IT, YOU CAN DO IT!
YOU CAN DO IT, YOU CAN DO IT, YOU CAN DO IT, YOU CAN DO IT!

CHAPTER 13:
DRAGON OF WISHES

"Step forward in trust, and watch your power unfold."

Installing 99%

The Dragon of Wishes

You left the Wise Man's house, his teachings leaving a heavy weight on your mind. **Questions flood your thoughts: "Where should I go? How do I find the Dragon of Wishes?"**

Suddenly, you remember the Oasis parable and the Wise Man's words.

"Depending on where you want to arrive, I'll be where the invisible is. Believe in the unseen, the invisible, the unknowable. But you'll always be closer if you act."

You: "Well, let me imagine that I have made this journey, and on a high mountain above the clouds, I am met by the majestic Dragon of Wishes."

After visualizing the picture in your mind, you notice the tallest mountain in the distance.

You: "I'm going there!"
You felt a strange tingling in your fingers as the Emerald Ring of the Wise Man suddenly began to glow with brilliant green light.

With a single step, you find yourself on the summit of a mountain. Thunder crashes overhead, and a platform of clouds forms beneath your feet. From the void, a deep voice rises, "This way!"

Your heart races as you realize you're walking on clouds. As you move forward, the Dragon of Wishes emerges, hovering in the air, its presence both serene and overwhelming. It greets you with a knowing, wise gaze filled with understanding and depth.

You *(lost your own ability to speak and asked the dragon)*:
"What does all this mean? How is this possible?"
The Dragon of Wishes: "Do you remember what the Wise Man told you? Thoughts lead to actions. Now, it has happened, though in a slightly different form than you might not have expected. Your beliefs and thoughts showed you the way, and the ring activated after you took the first step. You believed in yourself, you believed you were the chosen one. You are already here because you believe. You are the creator."

You *(stunned, whispering)*:
"I... I'm the creator?"
The Dragon of Wishes *(nodded)*:
"Notice, throughout the journey, logic doesn't quite add up, events become increasingly abstract. This world, this moment it has always been your dream. Now, as you stand on the edge of its meaning, you awaken to its truth."

The Dragon of Wishes began to shimmer, transforming into streams of golden light until it disappeared in a cloud of sparks. A silence filled the air with meaning. Slowly, the sparks began to shift and swirl, forming Heaven's Gate in the clouds, its golden edges glowing softly, as if it had always been waiting for you.

From somewhere unseen, a soft melody filled the air. It carried no words, only a feeling, a promise of something greater, of an end that was also a beginning. The gate stood open, radiant and inviting, its light pulling you forward.

Everything you knew, everything you had seen, begins to fade... and in the silence, a whisper calls, "Wake up."

HOW TO TURN DREAMS INTO REALITY

WAKE UP!

|NewReality|_01001101

[REBOOT]_newperspective

Installing 100% 

<THINK>_different_01010111

///_Congratulation

>AwakenMind_01101011<

<<LEVEL_UP>>_00111001

LAUNCH!

The Daily Morning Question to Transform Your Life:

*What would the person
I want to become do today?*

Installed ✓✓

"One day or day one, you decide."

— Paulo Coelho

"Share this message, uplift others, and create change.
Together, we grow. Mention @mylifexsoul in your story!"

Part of Wealth is mindset.

One of the most profound moments of my life was when **I realized that life itself is a question, and how we live it serves as our answer.** The way we frame the questions we ask ourselves shapes the answers that ultimately define our lives.

If your inner voice is asking, "How?" it's a sign you're stepping beyond your comfort zone. **Remind yourself, "I'm learning, I'm growing, and I have the strength to make it happen!"**

Your "HOW?" will fade away once you start taking action.

"Share this message, uplift others, and create change. Together, we grow. Mention @mylifexsoul in your story!"

RECOMMENDATIONS

Understanding yourself better can be done through a variety of tests and exercises. Here are some popular tests:

- **16 Personality Test (Free version)**

Based on the Myers-Briggs Type Indicator (MBTI), it sorts you into one of 16 personality types. It helps you understand your strengths, weaknesses, and how you interact with others. This free version is a valuable tool for personal growth, career advice, and relationships. It can also help others understand you by revealing your natural tendencies and how you approach the world.

- **Holland Code Career Quiz (Free version)**

It helps you discover your career preferences by matching your interests to six personality types: Realistic, Investigative, Artistic, Social, Enterprising, and Conventional (RIASEC). This test can guide you toward career paths that fit your natural strengths and interests, leading to greater fulfillment and success in your professional life.

- **Wheel of Life Exercise (Free version)**

It is a self-assessment tool that allows you to evaluate key areas of your life, such as career, health, relationships, finances, and personal growth. Rating your satisfaction in each area on a scale from 1 to 10 helps you visualize where you're thriving and where more attention may be needed. This powerful exercise promotes balance, guiding you to set meaningful goals and work towards a more harmonious, purposeful, and fulfilling life.

Unique Journeys in Inspirational Cinema

1) **The World's Fastest Indian** · 2005 · Sport/Adventure
2) **Joy** · 2015 · Comedy/Drama
3) **The Founder** · 2016 · Documentary/Action
4) **The Intern** · 2015 · Comedy/Drama
5) **The Banker** · 2020 · Drama
6) **The Billionaire** · 2011 · Comedy/Drama (Thailand)
7) **Harley and the Davidsons** (TV Mini Series 2016)
8) **Adidas vs. Puma** · 2016 · Drama/History
9) **Mr. Nobody** · 2009 · Sci-fi/Fantasy
10) **The Bucket List** · 2007 · Comedy/Adventure
11) **The King's Speech** · 2010 · Drama/Indie film
12) **Seven Pounds** · 2008 · Romance/Thriller
13) **Big Eyes** · 2014 · Crime/Comedy
14) **Bleed for This** · 2016 · Sport/Drama

15) **Jobs** · 2013 · Drama/Indie film
16) **The Pursuit of Happyness** · 2006 · Family/Drama
17) **Persian Lessons** · 2020 · War/Drama
18) **Into the Wild** · 2007 · Adventure/Drama
19) **Rocket Singh: Salesman of the Year** · 2009 · Comedy/Drama
20) **Jerry Maguire** · 1996 · Comedy/Romance
21) **The Imitation Game** · 2014 · Thriller/War
22) **Concussion** · 2015 · Sport/Thriller
22) **The Playlist** · 2022 · Drama · 1 season
23) **Pay It Forward** · 2000 · Romance/Drama
24) **Yes Man** · 2008 · Comedy/Romance
25) **Tetris** · 2023 · Thriller/History
26) **The Two Popes** · 2019 · Comedy/Drama

27) **Whiplash** · 2014 · Indie film/Music
28) **King Richard** · 2021 · Sport/Drama
29) **An Interview with God** · 2018 · Mystery/Thriller
30) **I Origins** · 2014 · Sci-fi/Romance
31) **Jerry & Marge Go Large** · 2022 · Comedy/Drama
32) **A Hologram for the King** · 2016 · Comedy/Drama
33) **The Truman Show** · 1998 · Comedy/Sci-fi
34) **The Terminal** · 2004 · Comedy/Romance
35) **Lamborghini: The Man Behind the Legend** · 2022 · Sport/Drama
36) **Ford v Ferrari** · 2019 · Sport/Action
37) **YOUR LIFE** · TODAY · Adventure/Action

Dariusz

The Author & The Story Behind the Book

11010110 10010111 11101100
Code Word: This Is Where It Began.
END OF CODE.

#creator

My name is Dariusz Romanovski, and I wrote this book at 25 years old. Perhaps this surprises you, and some might think it's early, but for me, it was a conscious decision. This isn't something that happened overnight. I've been on this path since I was a teenager, and it has been full of curiosity, changes, and dreams that have shaped who I am today.

As a child, I remember praying for people and the world. I prayed that each person would be heard, that their requests would be heeded.

But the most profound moment came when I sincerely asked God for strength. Life immediately became a challenge, and that's when I realized the strength I was seeking was already within me, waiting to be unleashed. It was a powerful lesson: **God said, "believe and receive."**

The real miracle began when I started thanking God not just for blessings but for challenges, lessons, and every opportunity to grow. I began to understand more deeply, and from that moment, I also prayed, **"God, act through me."**

God said, "believe and receive."

As I went further into myself, the more I realized that everything I was experiencing was part of a larger picture, a spiritual journey shaping my soul. But everything connected to my childhood dream.

I dreamed of leaving an inspiring legacy, passing down something meaningful that would resonate through generations. I believe that life's events are woven together to create a chain of inspiration. When you pass it on to others, a part of you stays in their hearts, and that's a legacy that lasts forever.

I believe that God has endowed me with all the talents and essence needed to fulfill this mission. The journey hasn't been easy, but **it is the meaning of my life.** I've often felt like an outcast, a lone ranger, invisible to most. Yet, I trust that someday, despite all the obstacles and misunderstandings I've faced, others will come to understand the deeper meaning of my life.

A Miracle at Birth

I was born on May 20, 2000, at 20:00 PM, a time when it seemed impossible, yet the timing itself feels like a miracle. Doctors struggled, and my mother and I held on until the evening, when the chief doctor, who wasn't even supposed to be there that day, walked in, took control of the situation, and said, "Why are you torturing her?" **His unexpected presence changed everything.** Even now, I remember my mom telling me how, when he began to help, it felt as if an angel had entered the room.

My father once told me that during this time, he had a conversation with God in his mind. God asked, "Do you believe in me?" And my father answered, **"I believe."** That's how I came into this world.

Years later, my father told me that when I first opened my eyes, he was struck by how deeply they seemed to look at the world, as if they held depth and hidden knowledge from beyond. **I don't know if that's true, but I've carried those words with me as a reminder.** They've guided me in creating my own story, always staying true to the belief in my strength and the legacy I want to leave.

No matter how true it may be, it serves as a reminder of the power of words. How much can sincerity truly influence the world?

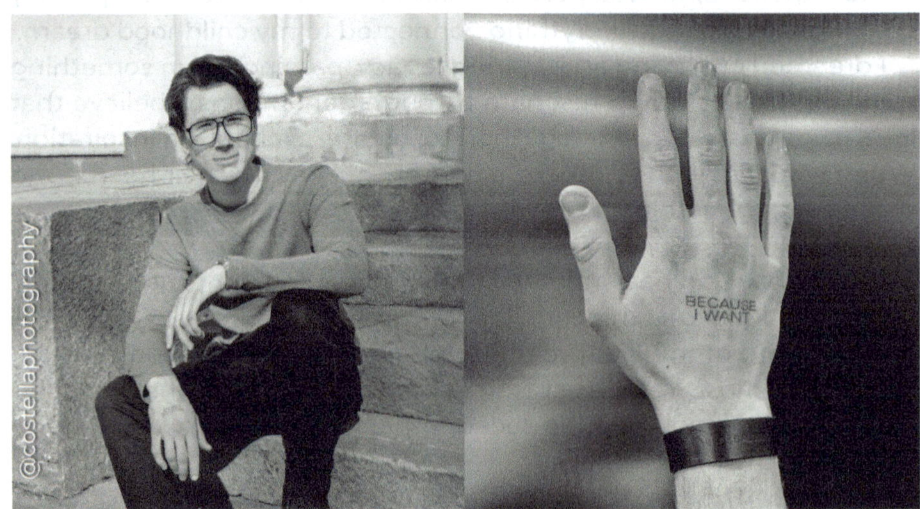

Turning Point

There was a time in my life when I struggled to find my place. As a child, I longed to fit in but often found myself on the outside. It was a challenging journey of searching for belonging while realizing that true growth comes from embracing who you are. Those struggles taught me that being different is not a weakness. It is a strength. Real power lies in staying true to your individuality, even when it's hard, uncomfortable, and challenging.

Years later, after serving in the Lithuanian Military Service, a decision I made to understand why others feared it and to discover with **curiosity** the lessons it held for me, I came to understand the depth of my desire, though it cost me my health and left me with a foot injury. Continuing my life journey, I explored different jobs, moving forward. It helped me discover more about who I truly was.

A turning point came when I decided to have foot surgery, a decision long postponed and uncertain. I remembered my father's words: **"I believe,"** and I made the decision, no matter what would happen. Lying in the operating room, embracing the unknown and looking at the flash of light above, I pondered life and what it truly represents, how fragile it is, yet **how beautiful it becomes when fully accepted as a game.**

Looking back, everything happened at just the right time. It marked the beginning of a profound change in my life. For the first time, I had the opportunity to reflect and rethink everything. It was during this time that I realized the **importance of being grateful** for the simple things in life, like the ability to walk, even through pain.

This experience shifted my perspective forever. It was as if I had gained new eyes, ones that allowed me to see life not just as a series of challenges, but as a series of lessons, all opportunities to grow and find deeper meaning. And in those moments of quiet reflection, I found peace in knowing that sometimes, it's the acceptance of **life's uncertainties that leads to the most profound change.**

A New Beginning - The First Attempt

This period of reflection gave birth to my book. What began as a personal project to help myself through a difficult moment **evolved** into something much bigger. The journey of writing became a way to **transform** my thoughts, stories, notes, emotions, and experiences into something meaningful and impactful.

During this process, I was in a flow, driven by passion. I spent hours on this project, sometimes even staying up until sunrise. Even when I woke up, the first thing I did was work on my book, not even thinking about eating. It felt like a healthy addiction, profoundly deeply connected to my soul. There were moments of uncertainty, but step by step, I kept moving forward. After all, I want to finish what I started. The path may not always be clear, but every step will bring you closer to where you want to be.

This book is like the voice of an angel in your life's journey at this stage, offering guidance and inspiration.

The first version of my book was a valuable learning experience. It wasn't perfect, but I dedicated my time, focus, passion, and faith to it. Even in the face of challenges and criticism, I ask myself what I can learn from them and push forward. This updated version reflects the lessons I've learned and the growth I've experienced. **Maybe this difficult and painful failure (lesson) was exactly what I needed to move forward.**

I'm truly proud of the direction it's taken and believe this version is the best representation of God's message through me. While the future is always a journey of learning, I'm excited to share this book with you, confident that it stands on its own and offers something truly personal and worthwhile.

Rebirth of the Book

With a **new outlook**, a **reignited sense of purpose**, and a **deep connection** to my **soul** and **heart**, I decided to rewrite and transform the book entirely. I also chose to **leave a part of myself** inside the book, including **my passion for motivating others**, as it has always been a core part of who I am.

This time, I infused the process with even more **passion**, **faith**, **gratitude**, and **purpose**, **dedicating** myself fully **to every detail**. With a renewed sense of clarity and determination, allowing the lessons from my past to guide me toward creating something truly meaningful. Now, it's ready to share with you, not just as a guide, but as a reflection of the journey that transformed me.

All these years, curiosity, the people I met along the way, gratitude, the highs and lows, but the choice to keep moving forward that's what shaped this book..

I invite you now to **ignite the fire within yourself**, to create your own masterpiece. Let this book be a part of God's presence in your heart, inspiring you to embrace your own unique journey. May it awaken the strength and potential you carry, reminding you that the **power to transform your life lies within you.**

Trust in your path, trust in your growth, and know that every step you take brings you closer to the person you are meant to be. As you walk this path, remember that **challenges are not obstacles but opportunities for growth.** Let every setback fuel your determination and every success remind you of the infinite possibilities ahead. Your journey is uniquely yours, and with every decision you make, you are shaping a future filled with purpose and fulfillment.

The **fire within you** is capable of lighting the way for others, so let your **light shine brightly**. Embrace your **power**, live with **intention**, and let your **actions** reflect the **vision** of the person you are becoming. This is your time, and the world is waiting for the **impact** only you can make.

Words to Actions, Actions to Art

Unexpectedly, while working through the process of organizing my thoughts for the Story Behind the Book, I ended up creating something more, an art piece, a reflection of who I am, shaped by both light and dark moments, and the creative journey process itself.

DARIUSZ ROMANOVSKI

As I once said, if I were a painting, I'd be alive with every stroke, filled with curiosity, a masterpiece in constant motion. This piece became a true symbol of life's unfolding journey, capturing the essence of growth, change, and evolution with each new chapter.

Life is a process of discovering the words hidden among the letters. When you uncover more words, you begin to feel the connection. **Words** evolve into **sentences**, sentences into **thoughts**, thoughts into **actions**, and actions into **results**. When you exhale and open your eyes, you become fully who you are and accept it within yourself, and that is beautiful.

1110001O 10101100 01110101
Code Word:
Create Your Future.
thank you !
Future
10111001 01110110 10010101
AUTHOR REVEALED. END OF CODE.
Code Word: You Matter.
PROCESS COMPLETE.
#creator

Invitation: The Dragon of Wishes

It's about a creative approach, using the **talents given by God**, and combining elements of my life, transformation, and knowledge into this creation.

The beautiful game and book, Start Game: The Magic of Goals.

Ultimately, the main goal of this book is to leave behind a legacy of inspiration for this generation and those to come, with the intention of reigniting your inner faith in yourself and your potential, which reflects faith in God, the unseen.

In life, choosing to truly hear yourself isn't about ease, but about challenges and growth. **Limitlessness is a reflection of your inner potential! Don't ever think that something is wrong with you** My results are a reflection of my choices and the circumstances that shaped them, and choosing to be open takes courage. But this time, no biography.

In the end, there's a moment in this book when the protagonist meets the Dragon of Wishes. But this dragon isn't a fearsome creature. It's a symbol of something greater, something beyond our struggles. This book represents the magic of setting goals, the power of transformation, and the soul's strength to rise above chaos. The Dragon of Wishes helps the protagonist realize that everything the protagonist has dreamed of can come true.

This isn't just a fantasy. It's a conscious decision to awaken and take control of your life. But remember to stay open to the Universe, to God, and allow them to be part of your journey. You can't control everything, so take action, embrace the journey, and keep gratitude in your heart along the way.

This book is more than just words on pages. It's a reflection of my journey, my challenges, and my unwavering determination to transform chaos into clarity.

It's not just a guide, it's a book with a soul, showing how your desires and goals can attract miracles into your life. The true key lies in realizing that we are more than our challenges and that within us is the unlimited strength to turn our dreams into reality.

Documenting My Journey: A Letter to My Future Self

One day, when I'm old, sitting in a rocking chair, enjoying the sun and greeting it with a wave of my hand.
I'll ask myself, Who am I?

And I'll answer, I am everything I dared to become!

Success is the courage to rise after every fall. If this book is one of my creations, then it's the result of those choices, of every moment I moved forward when it would have been easier to stop.

When I realized I am a creator, everything in life shifted. The talents and gifts placed within me were no longer just possibilities. They became tools I could use!
As long as I'm alive, I can create, and what I create becomes more than just mine. It becomes a piece of the world, part of its ongoing story.

I write this now at 24, documenting my thoughts not only for today but for the years ahead. Twenty-five years from now, I'll look back on these words, reflecting on where they led me and what new paths unfolded.

We are all connected by the things we give and the marks we leave behind. Do not underestimate what surrounds you, but most importantly, what is inside you.

Let soul live and heart beat in everything you do.

2025.01.11

10010110 11111010 10100111
Code Word: Believe.

Dariusz Romanovski

Wake Up and Win: 8 Steps to Win the Day!

- **Wake Up Early (or whenever works for you):**

We all have 24 hours in a day, and how we use them is entirely up to us. If you truly want to achieve your goals, be willing to exchange some of your sleep for time dedicated to goals. How you manage your time today will shape your future.

- **Hydrate:**

Drink a glass of warm water to rehydrate your body after sleeping.

- **Stretch and Warm-Up:**

Do some light stretches to wake up your muscles, then get your blood flowing with a few minutes of activity.

- **Mental Clarity:**

Take a shower to help clear your mind, relax, and reset before diving into your tasks for the day.

- **Connect with Yourself:**

1. Find a quiet, peaceful space where you can sit comfortably without distractions.
2. Close your eyes, take slow, deep breaths and center yourself.
3. Focus your attention on your breath, feeling each inhale and exhale as it grounds you. If your mind starts to lose focus, gently guide it back to your breath.

- Repeat positive affirmations such as:

4. **"I am confident," "I am ready for the day," "I will achieve my goals."** Let these affirmations resonate deeply, strengthening your sense of purpose for the day ahead.

- **Healthy Breakfast:**

Start your day with a nutritious breakfast full of protein, fiber, and healthy fats. We are what we eat, so fuel your body and mind for success. Healthy salads are great for focus.

- **Review Your Goals:**

Take a moment to review the 3 tasks from your set goal that you planned the evening before. Writing them down again in the morning isn't just helpful, it's essential. This simple action sharpens your focus and reactivates your system, bringing you closer to accomplishing your goals.

- **Get Ready:**

Dress in clothes that make you feel good, and get ready to crush the day. You've got this! You are SUPERHERO!

Evening Rituals for a Winning Tomorrow!

- **Reflect on Your Day:**

Dedicate 10-15 minutes each evening to reflect on your day. Celebrate your wins, no matter how small, and recognize the opportunities for growth. Keep in mind, what gets measured, gets improved. Progress is made one step at a time, and by focusing on consistent, small efforts, you'll create the momentum for lasting transformation.

- **Review Your Goals for Tomorrow:**

Review your tasks for the next day and prioritize the top 3. Writing them down creates a clear roadmap and ensures you start your day with purpose, focus, and ready to take decisive action toward your chosen goal.

- **Avoid Screens:**

Give your mind a chance to relax by staying away from phones, computers, or TV for at least 30 minutes before bed. This simple habit helps you calm down and prepares you for restful sleep, setting the stage for a productive tomorrow.

- **Plan for Tomorrow:**

Prepare for success by organizing everything you'll need for the next day, from your clothes to your meals to your workspace. This simple step the night before can reduce stress and ensure a smoother, more productive start in the morning.

- **Practice Gratitude:**

Before bed, reflect on 3 things you're grateful for. This simple practice helps shift your mindset, reduce stress, and set the tone for a peaceful night's sleep, leaving you refreshed, focused, and and ready to greet the day with faith and purpose.

- **Bonus:**

End your day with the powerful motivational audios from Ben Lionel Scott's channel to set the tone for an even more successful tomorrow. You know what?

You're a winner!

If you had your own quote,
what would it be?

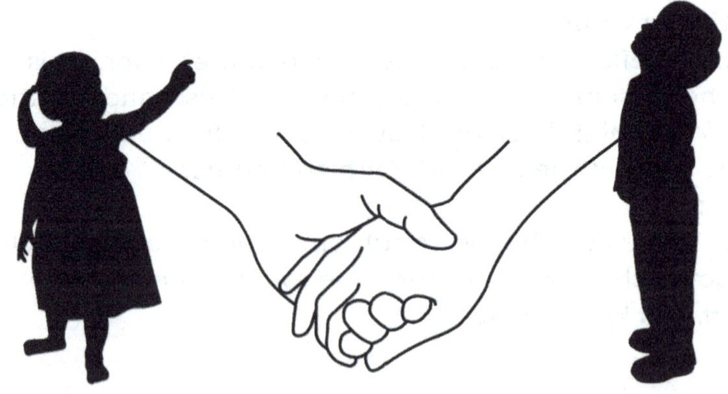

"Share this message, uplift others, and create change. Together, we grow. Mention @mylifexsoul in your story!"

Letter for You:
Own Today, Shape Tomorrow.

Dear Soul, Thank you for walking this journey with me.
Every step you take through these pages brings you closer to unlocking your full potential.

Remember, the smallest changes can lead to the greatest transformations. Even when the road seems difficult, you are shaping the person you are meant to become.

Change is never easy but it is always possible. Every challenge, every moment of doubt, and every silent battle you fight within yourself is part of your growth. Your strength lies in your ability to keep moving forward even when the path ahead is uncertain.

This book is not an answer but a beginning. A spark that I hope will ignite something within you. Every goal begins with fear. But once you overcome it, the journey truly begins. In the end, it is not the goal itself that shapes us, but the path we take to reach it. I hope this book has helped remove fear and obstacles from your life, leaving only an open door to your dreams and goals. Because once fear is left behind, the journey becomes an adventure, not just a destination. Your dream is closer than it seems, waiting for you to step into it.

But how should I live in the present moment? The answer lies in the balance between conscious action and trust in the process. In your ability to silence the noise of the world and listen to your own voice. In your courage to embrace change, express yourself boldly, and trust your intuition.

There will be moments when the world moves in a different rhythm. Do not let this shake you. When others give in to the chaos, you will remain grounded in your vision. Trust that the way to lasting success is carved not in following the crowd, but in honoring your unique journey, one step at a time. Isolation is not being alone. It's the space where you reconnect with your true self, free from distractions.

The quiet moments are where clarity is born. Discipline is about aligning your actions with your highest potential. Focus is not about avoiding the world, but about immersing yourself fully in the things that truly matter. These are the principles that will carry you forward in your pursuit of lasting success.

And you might ask me, why go through all this when it's easier to simply enjoy life? Perhaps the answer lies in being true to yourself, finding joy, and discovering meaning in the process itself. When we embrace the journey, rather than chase fleeting moments, we discover fulfillment that lasts beyond temporary pleasures. The choices I make today will one day serve as an example, a guiding light for others seeking their own way. They are not just actions, but seeds planted for a future that holds meaning—both for me and for those who observe. What we do now echoes beyond our own lives, inspiring others to pursue their own truth, to embrace their potential, and to realize that their journey, too, is worth every step.

The world does not just need more people chasing success. It needs leaders who inspire others through their actions and way of life. When you choose to rise above instant gratification and pursue something greater, you begin to understand that true success is built on a foundation of purpose, consistency, and vision.

Own your journey, never wait for permission to dream or approval to rise. You are already worthy, already enough, and already capable of more than you ever thought possible. Each of us has the ability to grow and evolve until our very last breath.

Keep moving! Keep growing! Keep becoming!
Your future is already unfolding. Walk boldly into it, make your choices, and understand why they were made.

With unwavering faith in your potential,

Dariusz Romanovski FAITH

Awaken to Limitless Potential!

My first version of this book, 1.0, written in 2024, was something I viewed as my personal child. I invested my time and effort into it, but it lacked something crucial: soul and purpose. The words were there, the foundation was set, but it didn't have that spark, that life.

Then I thought when God breathed life into us through the soul, He didn't just give us existence. He gave us limitless potential. He gave us the power to be fully alive, to create, to evolve, and to awaken to our true selves.

Just like that, this book has evolved. It's no longer just words on a page. **It's a living testament to the power of transformation.** This book is about awakening to your true potential, letting your soul guide you to new heights, and becoming more than you ever thought possible..

Just as I've transformed this book, know that you too have the power to awaken and evolve. Your potential is limitless!

If you found this book helpful, please leave a review and share or gift it to someone you think it could help.
Your support can make an impact. Thank you!

YOU'RE WEALTHY!

Sometimes we think we need more knowledge, but what we really lack is the confidence to take a step with what we already have. **New information without action becomes a weight, holding us back instead of moving us forward.** The world won't be perfect, and the answers won't all appear. But it's the act of moving forward that brings clarity and opens doors to what you're searching for.

Trust yourself and your decisions, even if they don't feel fully planned. True progress comes from action, not waiting for the *"perfect"* moment or the *"right"* advice. Use what you already know and put it into action, even if it feels small or imperfect. Take the insights from this book and apply them in your life. You'll be amazed at how those first steps can spark momentum, shift your mindset, and move you closer to the life you've always imagined. Each action builds confidence, and with every step forward, you're creating the change you've been looking for.

www.magicofgoal.com

"Share this message, uplift others, and create change. Together, we grow. Mention @mylifexsoul in your story!"

FOR SOMEONE SPECIAL:
WRITE A WISH, INSPIRE A DREAM!

THE MAGIC PAGE:
DREAM. WRITE. ACHIEVE!

Reflect on what you've learned and write your next steps toward making your dreams come true:

Made in the USA
Monee, IL
01 May 2025